DIRECTOR'S CHOICE
SLOVAK NATIONAL GALLERY

SLOVAK NATIONAL GALLERY

Alexandra Kusá

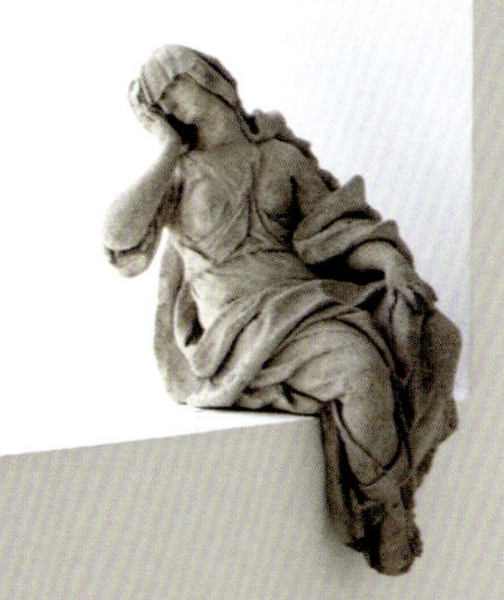

INTRODUCTION

The Slovak National Gallery, founded in 1948 a few months after the establishment of the Communist Party government, is one of Europe's youngest national galleries. Its relative 'institutional youth', together with the search for (and subsequent adaptation of) a suitable site for its premises, broadly determined the character and policy of the organisation. In the newly socialist Czechoslovakia, the Slovak National Gallery was conceived of as an emblematic institution of the smaller of the two 'fraternal republics'. Its foundation took place against the backdrop of an emerging cultural policy

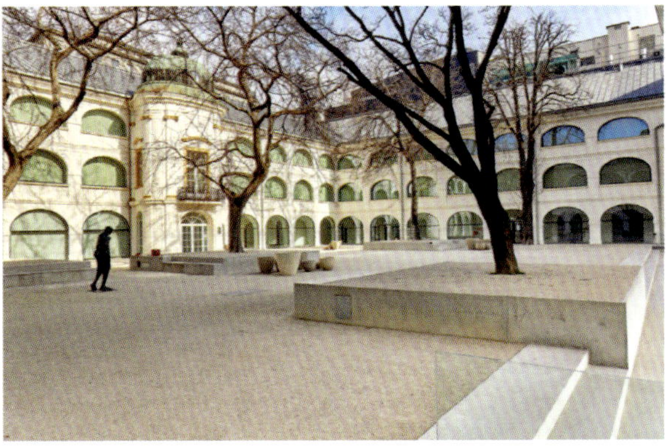

of socialist realism which, together with the desire to build a base, directed its development – for better and for worse. The positive aspect of the gallery's youth was that for its specialist staff the issues of institutional development and creating a professional workplace were always placed above any pursuit of current cultural policy. The gallery therefore succeeded in building collections that reflected the breadth of Slovak art and avoided becoming merely an agent of the prevalent ideology, although it came under constant political pressure.

Most collections are unsurprisingly devoted to twentieth-century domestic art. However, political influence propelled the building of an important collection of medieval sacred art long regarded as the jewel in the gallery's crown. To eliminate the role of religion, the state promoted transfer of works of art from church estates to museum collections – the sacred was to become the museological. Another important element was a struggle over the physical form of the gallery, beginning with the romantic Water Barracks building. This was far from a traditional European museum, a point underscored by the open arcade courtyard with its evidently festive rather than monumental atmosphere. The founding director, Karol Vaculík, was thus faced with an inspirational task: to build a national gallery on a green field – both physically and ideologically. The defining factor was that from the outset he moved towards precincts and a comprehensive workplace. As it was not a palace building, he was not burdened by sentiment but was instead free to opt for a modern solution.

The architect of the gallery's physical form (1969) was Vladimír Dedeček. He designed the area around the Water Barracks, a distinctive neomodern building on the Danube embankment. Unfortunately, the proposal was too complex for the capacity of the socialist economy and beyond the will of cultural policy. Only part of Dedeček's proposed design was ever completed. The entrance, together with the bold architecture inserted into the historicist street line, did not align with community expectations and was never implemented. The public of the 'progressive socialist state' was extremely conservative and the gallery became a reviled building – with its red panelling, it was even seen as a symbol of communism. This was particularly evident following the collapse of the regime in 1989, when most within the professional community and the public demanded its redevelopment. The gallery's management team

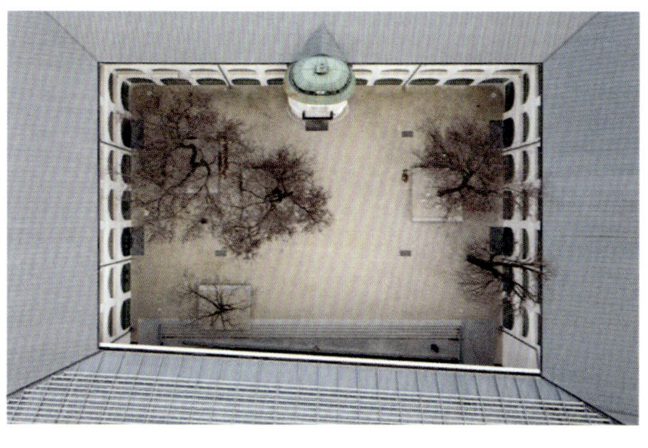

devoted significant effort to its preservation and subsequent reconstruction, which was completed in 2022. We have now been operating the building for two years, learning in the process, and through experience are attempting to define what an art museum is – or can be – in the twenty-first century.

We do not view ourselves as a museum that preserves collections, but as a cultural institution that facilitates enjoyment of quality leisure time for its visitors – whether at an exhibition, through a programme or 'as it comes' on the banks of the Danube. Equally important to us is our role as an actor in social debate, which is why we prepared several pioneering exhibitions on problematic periods of our history: *Art and Propaganda 1939–1945, Art of Socialist Realism, Photography 1969–1989, Akcia Zet* and others. My colleagues and I have been wondering what constitutes our iconic work, our *Mona Lisa*, and thanks to this book I finally know. It is our premises on the Danube embankment, the architectural edifice that reflects physically what we are trying to do conceptually: to update the past.

MARKO BLAŽO (1972–2021)

Genealogy 2. 2009
Digital print on paper, 60 × 80 cm
Purchased in 2011. G 13556

The artist was a star of the generation that entered the scene at the end of the 1990s – the decade shortly after the revolution, when society was still curious about new forms of art and the creativity of the young. Back then Blažo's presentations, such as bubble-gum 'paintings', various surreal objects and situational 'gaming' installations, were immediately recognised for their distinctive poetics. It was a rich, romantic, yet melancholic world. The artist worked with numerous genres, and an important aspect for him was an idea that he developed through various media – creating objects, paintings and installations. Although Blažo depicted the world around him, it is a world that transcends rules – a world of inverted logic, filled with paradoxes applied to ordinary situations, motives and themes. Within his works, successive plans are repeatedly layered and coded. On this journey, he drew on his sense of the absurd, an increasing self-irony, knowledge of art history and echoes of the nostalgic land-scape of his childhood.

Blažo overturned the territory of memories and cognition and imposed upon it new rules. He built a world in which a stork merges with a unicorn, a church sleeps in a bed and a cabbage mutates into a brain – as it does in this work. I selected him because, along with my colleague, we staged his first solo exhibition – the first for him and for us. In 2022 we acquired from his estate a significant volume of his works and this year (2024) we prepared his first retrospective. Marko Blažo is, in short, 'our' emblematic artist of the 1990s.

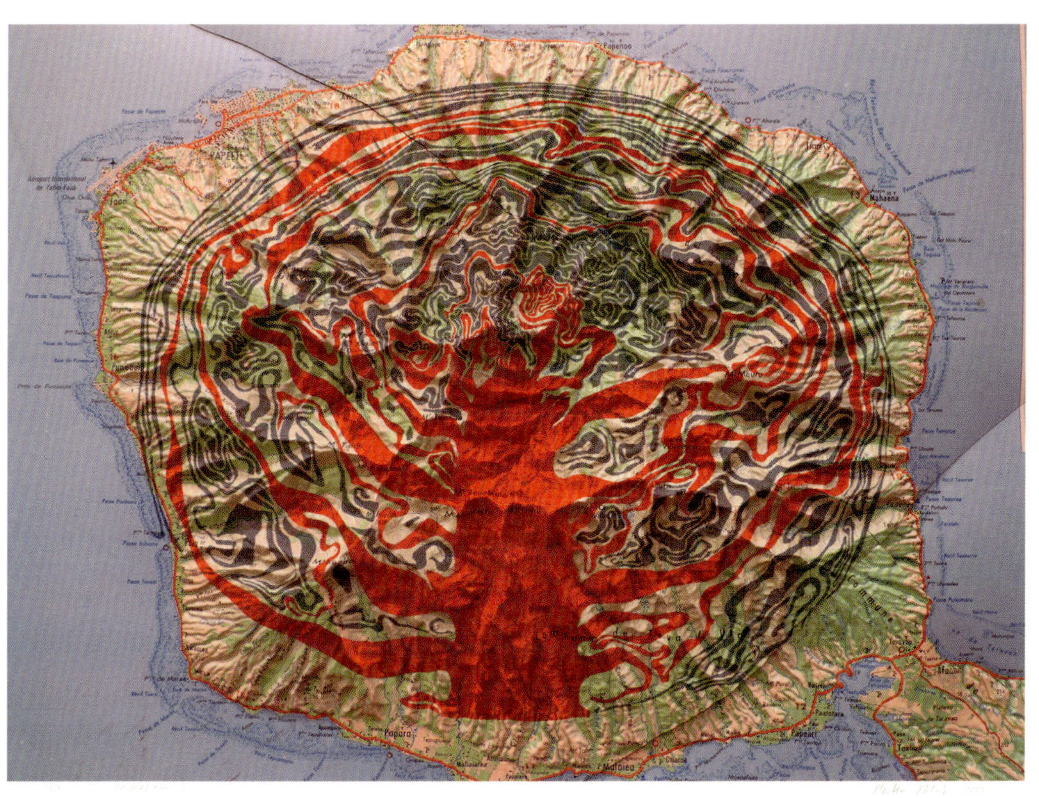

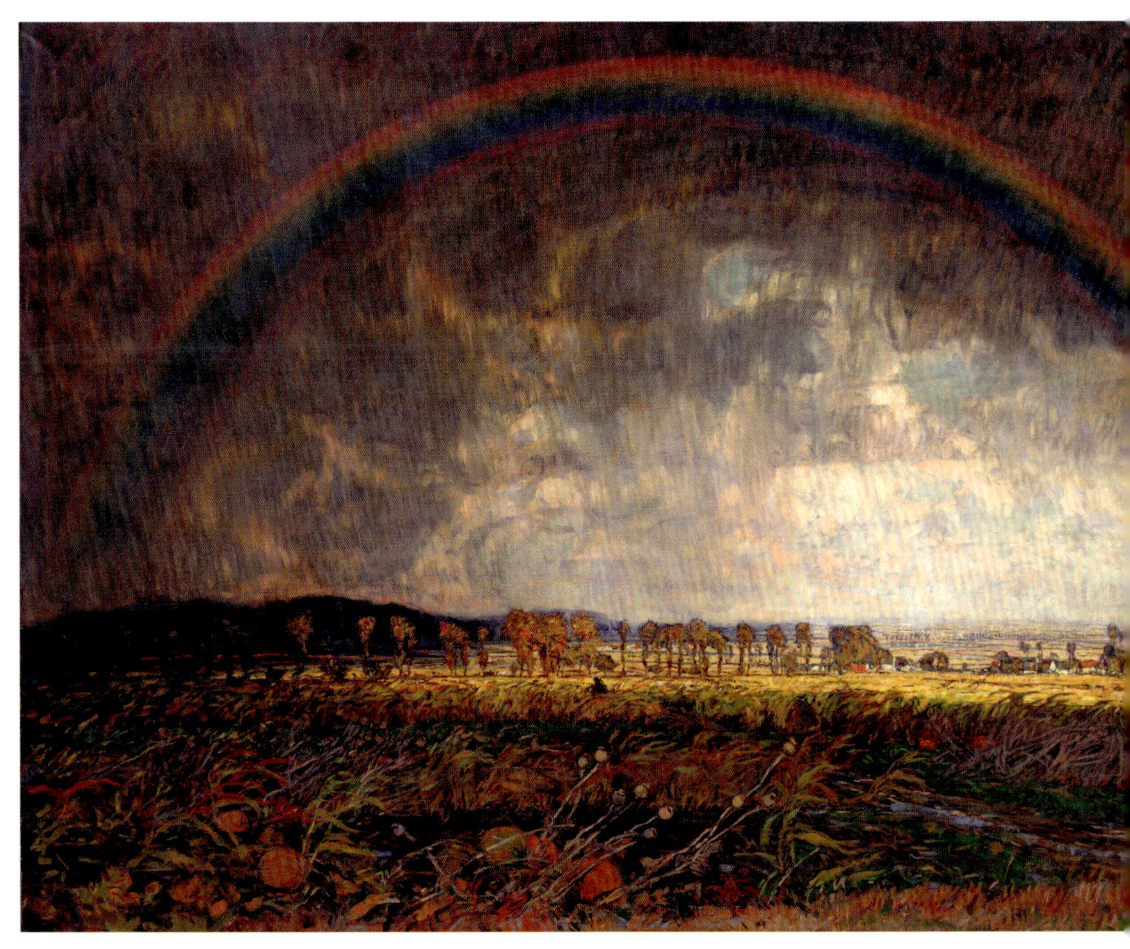

MARTIN BENKA (1888–1971)

Rainbow (After a Storm). 1918

Oil on canvas, 121 × 170 cm

Purchased in 1949. O 1

The artist is a founding figure of Slovak modern painting and a key representative of what we now call the 'Slovak myth' – that is, visualisations of various ideas within the Slovak community about itself, actually various forms of visual exploration to define and grope for our own identity. That is why Benka's work is still considered an expression of 'national style' and has been exploited by every regime. It is a historical paradox that the artist discovered his Slovak theme from Prague when beginning to visit Slovakia, whose contemporary exoticism of the departing world he transferred almost like a hymn onto his canvases. The world of statuesque shepherds, heroic woodcutters and romantic rafters, all set against a backdrop of layered patterns of bluish mountains with veils of mist and clouds, became an integral part of the visualisation of 'Slovakness'.

The selected painting, however, does not belong to this set. It is chosen for another reason – it is entered in the gallery's inventory as O 1, i.e. as the first painting. The inventory was created only after the first set of works was assembled, so we can assume that our colleagues did this deliberately. The 1918 work subsequently received another title, *After a Storm,* and it is beyond doubt that not only the entry in the inventory but also the title refer symbolically to the optimism associated with the end of the First World War and the subsequent establishment of the young democratic republic in 1918. Today, the symbolism of this work takes on a profound additional dimension.

JURAJ ŠAJMOVIČ (1932–2013)

War Generation. 1952

Black and white photograph, 28.5 × 38.5 cm

Acquired as a gift in 1991. UP-DK 1714

I have long hesitated over which photograph to choose. I considered a classic modernist composition from the 1930s; the history of photography abounds with them, and they are all beautiful. Yet finally I opted for this image, which better represents our collections. It reflects their long-term development and provides a reference to important projects that, while mapping the domestic history of photography, also gave visual testimony to the times we lived through. The exhibitions and catalogues *Lost Time?*, *Captivated by Beauty* and *New Slovakia* are also a pictorial report on the country and its people. This image and the current situation in Ukraine beautifully confirm this, and it is particularly disarming to know that behind the lyrical idyll of sitting in the grass is a society emerging from a drastic conflict. We see a generation prescribed to live under socialism, a generation that lost its freedom before it could comprehend it. Since it is my parents' generation, this photograph also has a special personal dimension for me.

In addition to photography, the artist worked professionally and successfully as a cinematographer, creating many successful films. His cinematic thinking is also evident in his images – he has a flair for the moment, and his photographs seem to be fragments of stories that we would like to know. Perhaps contributing to this was his family's destiny – both Czechoslovak and Central European – stretching from Piešt'any through Budapest to Prague; even as they fled persecution and injustice, they sought to confront this with their work and their creativity.

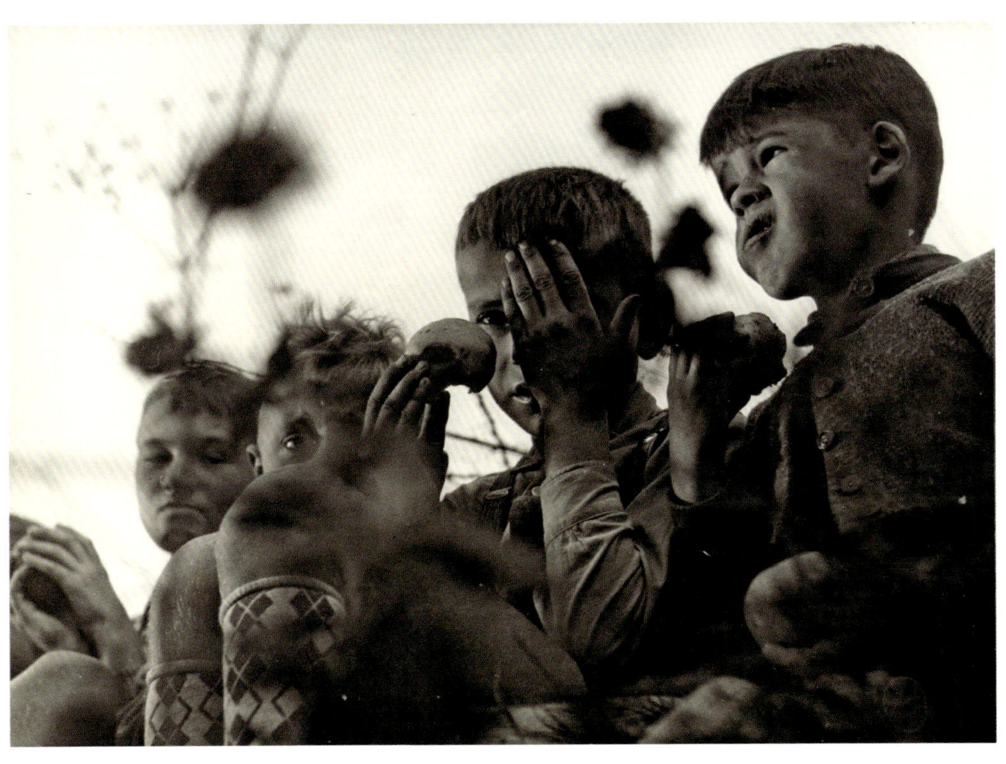

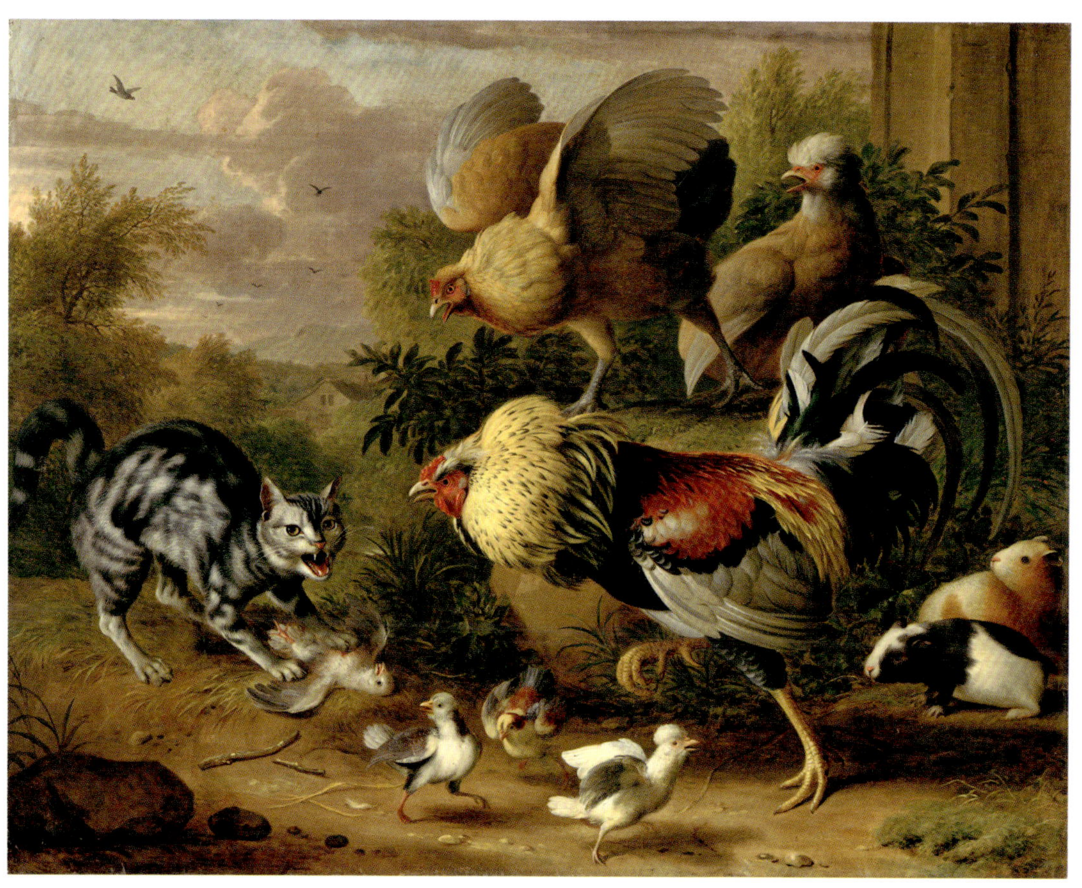

JAKUB BOGDAN (BOGDANI; around 1660–1724)

Cat among Roosters. 1706–10

Oil on canvas, 103.5 × 126 cm
Purchased in 1949. O 3

Jakub Bogdan, a painter originally from Prešov in eastern Slovakia, as one of the few artists of the then – and let us admit, also today's – periphery of Europe, built a decent career close to the English royal court. Our painting, more accurately a pair of paintings since it also includes the scene of the *Cockfight* (SNG O 2), belongs to Bogdan's English period. Their iconography draws on the animal or hunting still lifes popular at the time, which largely belonged to the repertoire of Dutch painters of the seventeenth-century 'golden age'. It is not surprising, then, that Bogdan was in Amsterdam at the end of his life. The Slovak painter has elevated the seemingly banal struggles of the farmyard into a literal fight to the death, including all the requisite actors: the aggressors, the defenders, the interested audience (one wonders what guinea pigs are doing in a poultry aviary), down to the casual 'passersby'.

Both paintings have additional importance to the Slovak National Gallery: as their inventory numbers indicate, they were among the first purchases for the nascent collections of the institution, which had been founded only a year before their acquisition in 1949. In a sense, they foreshadowed the subsequent (and perhaps current) mission of our institution: to nurture quality regional art, but on a supra-regional scale. As documented by the bidding (and results) from several recent world auctions, Bogdan suits these attributes perfectly.

ĽUDOVÍT FULLA (1902–1980)

Devín. 1930

Oil on canvas, 70 × 80 cm
Acquired as a transfer in 1961. O 1927

This artist is an icon of Slovak art. He entered the scene in the 1920s and represents the typical story of a modern painter who passed through all the -isms and finally found his own distinctive style, one in which he merged the European with the Slovak. After the 1930s Fulla's work combined in a particular way practices inspired by contemporary European avant-garde painting, folk art, children's artistic expression, icon painting and medieval art. The result was an original artistic language, notable for its synthesis of rational constructive structural form and intense emotive colour. As a modernist, he was initially denounced in the communist period, during which time he illustrated Slovak fairy tales and became a frame of reference for generations of children.

Fulla is also the 'domestic' artist of our gallery. In the 1960s he donated his work to the state, in return for which a gallery with an apartment was built for him. The gallery and works, together with the brutalist tomb of the painter and his wife, are now in the care of our gallery, as they were during his lifetime. The Fulla Gallery was the only building in the entire republic constructed to meet the needs of contemporary art – a bold building in a distinctly traditional environment. Fulla later returned to his native Liptov, where he devoted himself to painting. The chosen painting, *Devín,* is not one that seeks to express 'Slovak essence', but it is a beautiful painting, a portrait of a special place with a symbolic character for us. It portrays a castle where the Morava River flows into the Danube; for me, this is a place of Czech–Slovak solidarity.

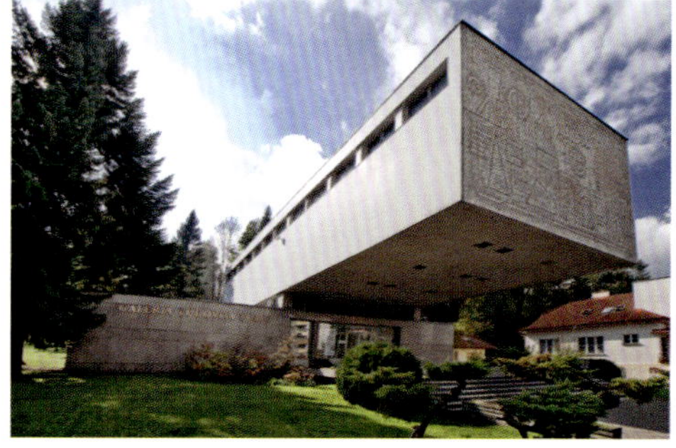

MARTIN KUSÝ: *Ľudovít Fulla Gallery in Ružomberok,* 1969

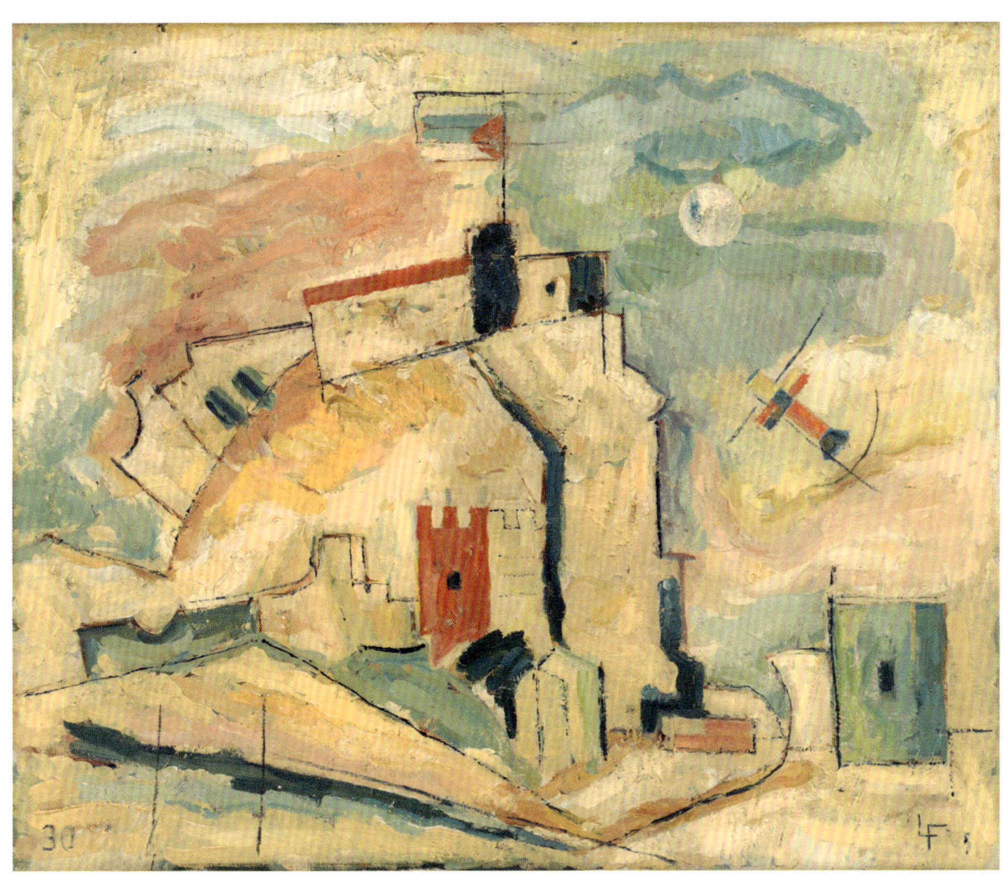

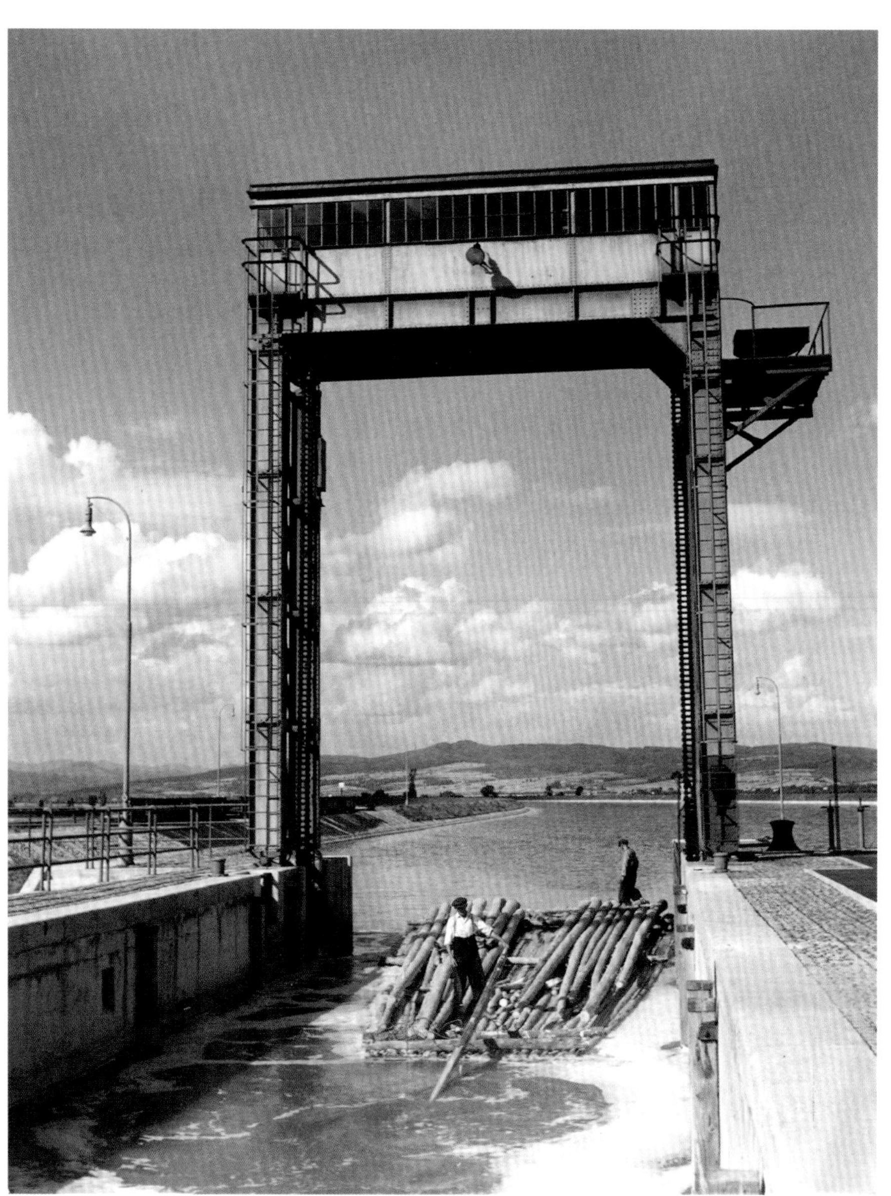

VILIAM MALÍK (1912–2012)

The Hydroelectric Power Station in Ladce. Around 1938

Black and white photograph on photographic paper, 39.8 × 29.8 cm

Purchased in 2010. UP-DK 3936

Malík was one of the most important representatives of modern photography in Slovakia. As a typical amateur photographer, he captured a wide range of subjects; professional photographers with creative ambition were practically non-existent in Slovakia at the time. This image is from the period of the Slovak state (a satellite state of Nazi Germany). Following its establishment, Malík's photographic interests changed – it was as if thematically he gradually moved, or escaped, from the modern city to the countryside. He struggled to accept that people from the social periphery disappeared as a theme or that forms of the modern city and attributes of contemporary civilisation had receded into the background – and that where they did appear it was in altered contexts of meaning.

Contrary to his intention, this photograph was embraced by the Slovak state. The picture shows two rafters cautiously manoeuvring their raft to pass through the enormous steel gates of the recently completed hydroelectric power station. The artist managed to capture not only the key moment of this event, but also the 'decisive' moment in the history of Slovakia. Not many photographs by Slovak artists capture such a clear turning point, one at which an entire civilisation inevitably gives way to another. Ultimately it became unsustainable to transport timber in this traditional way.

Despite the photograph having been taken earlier, Slovak state propaganda portrayed it as a symbol of the building of the 'New Slovakia'. This dramatic moment became a symbol of the dynamism of the young Slovak state, resulting in frequent publication in the press. The only retrospective exhibition of the artist was held in our gallery in 2013.

MILOŠ ALEXANDER BAZOVSKÝ (1899–1968)

Axe. 1952

Oil on canvas, 90 × 70 cm
Purchased in 2013. O 6995

The artist is an icon and a representative of the second modern wave of Slovak painting. He is also my favourite painter from the generation that adopted the aesthetic doctrine of looking for a modern form of 'Slovakness', but did so critically, or rather polemically, as evidenced by Bazovský's works. Of all Slovak painters, he was the most affected by the totalitarian climate of the 1950s. The artist never managed to work in accordance with the doctrine of socialist realism. He genuinely could not paint against his convictions because painting for him was more than a task, more than a way of depicting the world; it was rather a prerequisite, a part of his personality.

Nevertheless, the premature conclusion of Bazovský's oeuvre, which includes *Axe,* is its universally acknowledged peak. During this period he began to articulate the shape and surface of painted objects more expressively, multiplying the effectiveness of his rendering of colour. Despite its lyrical presentation, however, this work has a critical dimension. The simple village motif is also a metaphor – a reference to a Slovak story in which a family mourns a child who could have been killed by a carelessly stowed axe in a storeroom, as nobody had thought to put it away. The axe thus also represents the idleness and insignificance of the 'common people', whose importance was unhealthily magnified after the communists came to power in the 1950s.

At a time when art was supposed to be 'combative', Bazovský managed to remain true to himself – an educated man with a sense of humour and irony. His rehabilitation was enthusiastically supported by the then director of our gallery, Karol Vaculík, who curated his first retrospective in 1961.

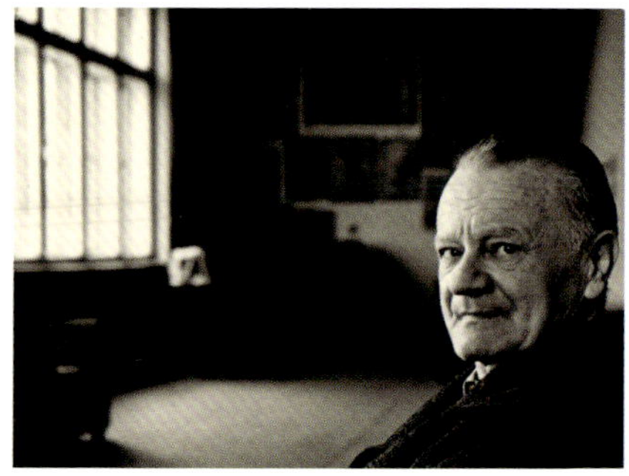

MAGDALÉNA ROBINSONOVÁ (1924–2006): *Miloš Bazovský. Portrait.* 1970. Black and white photograph, 43 × 56.5 cm. Purchased in 1970. UP-DK 485

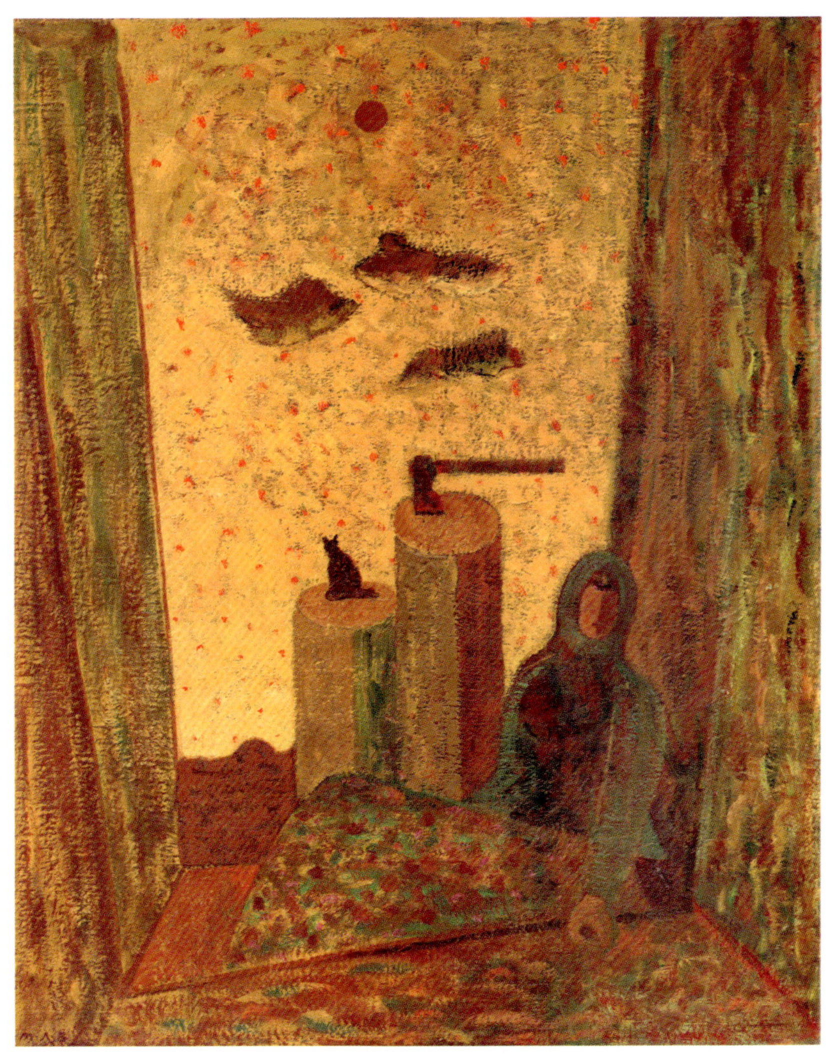

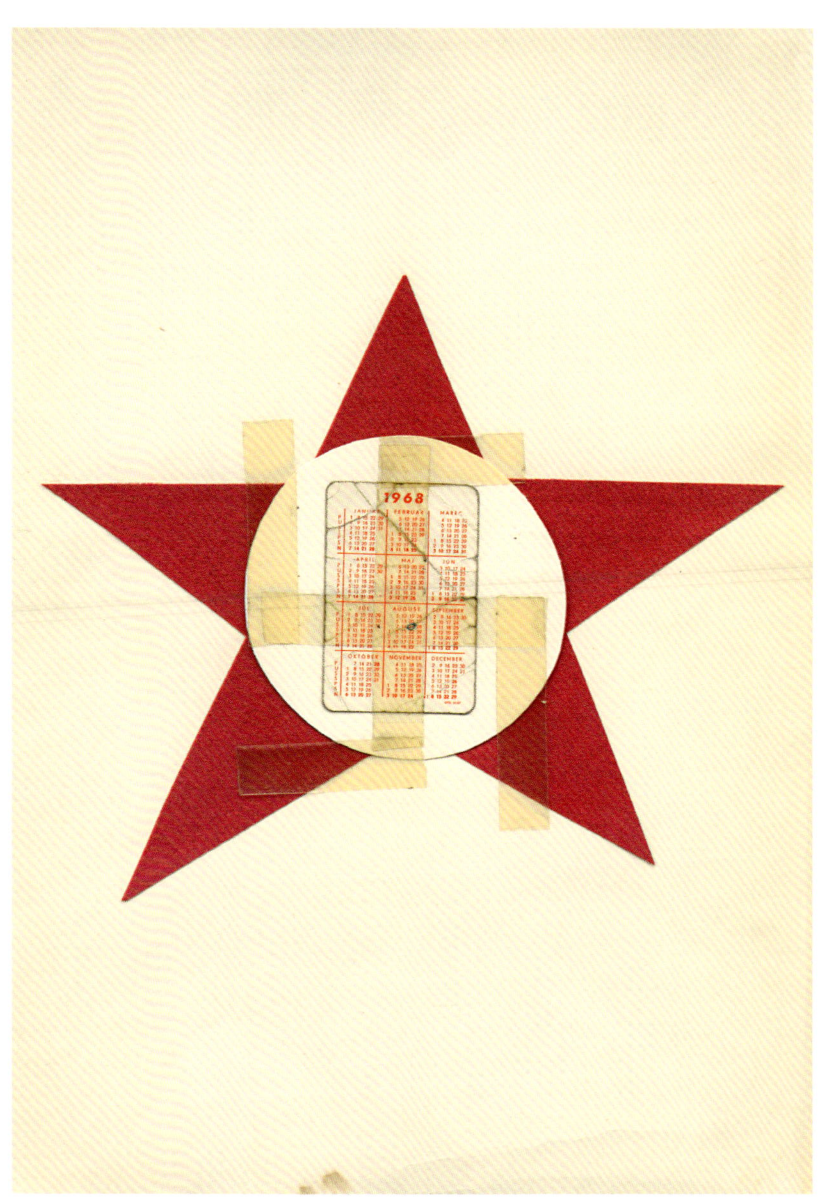

1968

JÚLIUS KOLLER (1939–2007)

Untitled (1968). 1968–75
Collage on paper, 45.3 × 31 cm
Acquired as a gift in 2009. IM 710

The artist belongs among the cult and defining figures of Slovak conceptual art. He is one of the few artists who beyond all doubt have transcended national recognition and established themselves within international circles. It is not art that dominates Koller's sphere of interest but culture, which has more power, more scope. His work is a persistent search to establish a space for art that does not consist simply of various ways in which to knead and distribute more or less beautiful matter.

In his series *Antipaintings,* Koller conducts a dialogue with a painting, analysing the image and altering the way in which we perceive it. He remains in a form of media interspace, known as a conceptualist and close to traditional painting, but not to illustrative painting. His expert curator Aurel Hrabušický has been working at the Slovak National Gallery for a long time, the reason why we became almost fatefully intertwined with his work. Currently we have the artist represented by *Antimuseum of J.K.* In its display, we exhibit a coherent collection of his works in private ownership.

We are also custodians of the Koller archive, which we have made available online – he is one of the emblematic artists of our gallery. For the selection, I chose a small work on paper that is unexpectedly brought to life by the international socio-political situation. With this collage from 1968, Koller reacted to the occupation of Czechoslovakia by Soviet troops – a subject that he pursued intensively throughout the period. The collage is based on a simple but eloquent abbreviated symbol, a principle that is his authorial trademark.

MARCEL MALIŠ (born 1978)

Thanks Seeming of the Czechoslovak People.
2020–21 (unfinished)
Acrylics on PVC, 870 × 800 cm
Painting event at the SNG

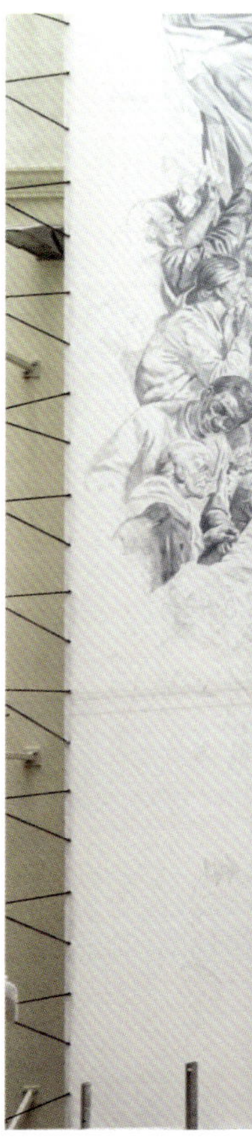

In November 2020, in the atrium of the National Gallery in Ester-házy Palace, artist Marcel Mališ began to paint an original replica of a lost work – *Thanksgiving of the Czech and Slovak People to Generalissimo Stalin* (1952), the icon of Czechoslovak socialist realism. How faithfully he approached the task was his decision. For the painter, the gallery was a 'workroom', and the painting thus emerged in the public eye. The painting event became the starting point for a new experimental genre – the art expedition – which we dedicated to thinking about the position of the national gallery as an educational institution for the modern day. We identified it as a place to ask questions and seek answers. For us, it was an opportunity to raise themes disturbingly present in our art (though not only there), especially the relationship between propaganda and art, hoaxes, the building of a cult of personality, the theme of fear, the relationship between the original and the copy, the issue of authorship, monumental creation, commissioned art, patronage and the perception and understanding of problematic aspects of our history.

The painting event was the backdrop for many educational activities for schools and the public, driven by our conviction that there is a path of experience and free discussion opposed to the dangers of totalitarianism. The painting is currently in a section of the gallery inaccessible to the public, awaiting its fate. Within his work, Marcel Mališ is an artist interested in interpretations of political events and the social 'body', as well as current trends of thought in philosophy and aesthetics; he does not shy away from the label of 'moralist'. Mališ is also represented in the gallery by other works.

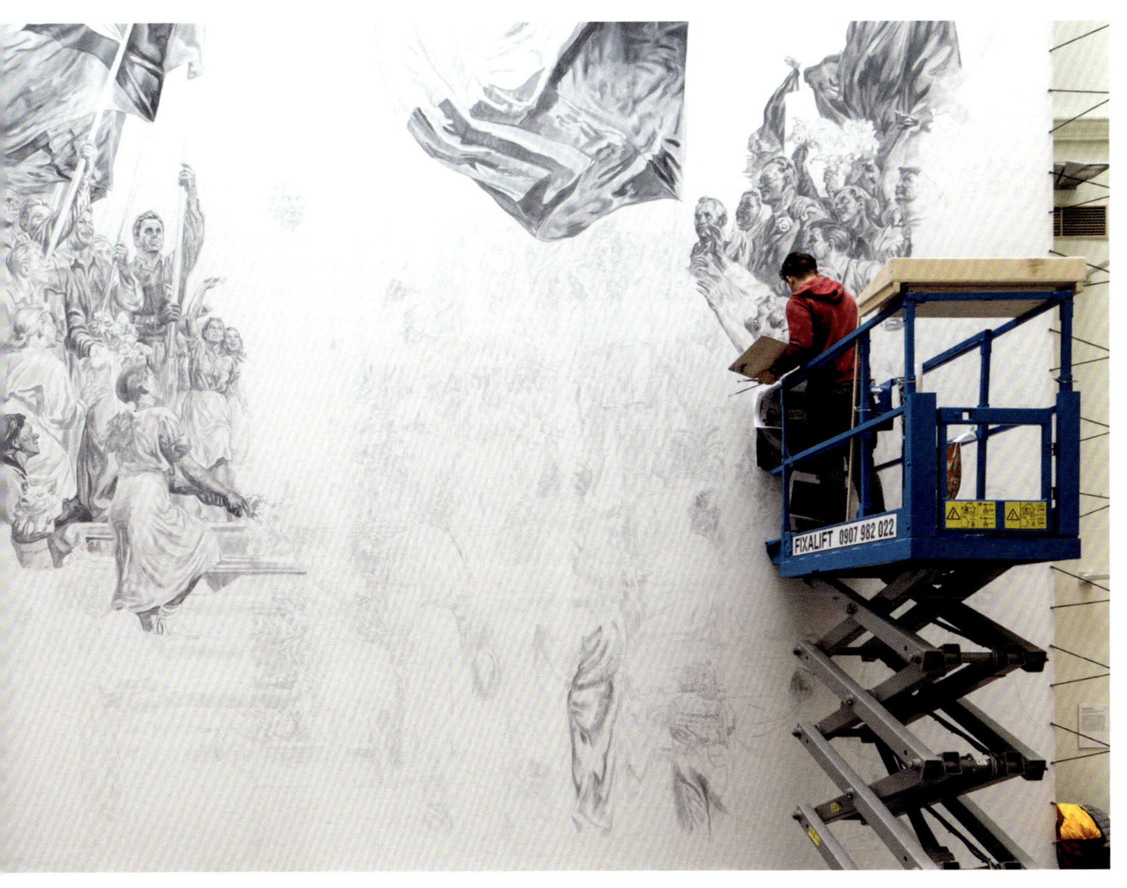

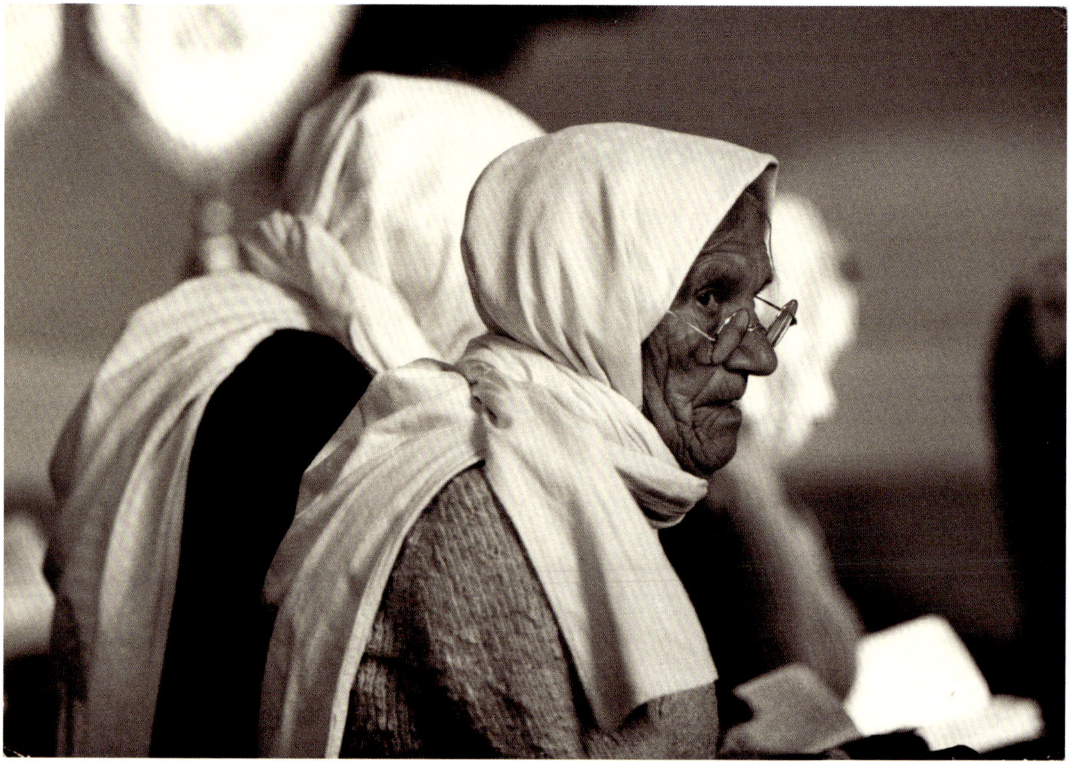

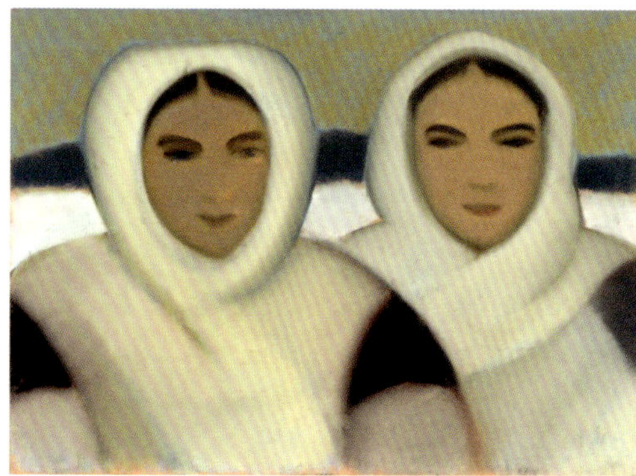

JANKO ALEXY (1894–1970):
Girls. 1932. Pastels on paper,
42 × 58.8 cm. Acquired as
a transfer in 1975. K 12506

MARTIN MARTINČEK (1913–2004)

In the Church IV. Around 1965

Black and white photograph, photographic paper, pasteboard, 42.8 × 59.5 cm

Acquired as a gift in 2002. UP-DK 3007

Martinček is one of the most important Slovak photographers of the second half of the twentieth century, although he took up photography by chance. Initially he studied law and served as a judge, but after a communist government was established he withdrew from this life and returned to his native region – picturesque Liptov. He lived there with Ester Šimerová-Martinčeková, an important Slovak modern painter. Perhaps thanks to her, he began to take photographs in the 1950s. He had no professional training, but had an intelligent and educated partner who knew modernism first hand from Paris.

A large body of Martinček's work comprises photography devoted to the image of the departing world, an aesthetic which at the Slovak National Gallery we refer to as 'Slovak myth'. We critically addressed the topic and prepared a thematic exhibition (2006) in which we identified it as a visual representation of the Slovak community's primary ideas about itself, about the meaning of its existence. These ideas often have a mythical dimension and are still politically exploited to revive long-defunct national identities. However, the Three Graces in the photograph are a movement in a different direction. The statuesque, almost archaic photograph of 'the Fates' in white is distorted by the intellectual spectacles, which serve subtly but pointedly to counter the myth. It mocks it, and yet the photograph remains truly beautiful.

In 2000 a large monographic exhibition of Martin Martinček's works was held at the Slovak National Gallery. Following the exhibition, the artist generously donated all photographs from the wider exhibition selection to our collections.

PAVOL ČEJKA – JAN ČUMLIVSKI – TOMÁŠ KLEPOCH

***In the Name of the Pentode –
Everything Is as It Really Is.*** 2014–18

Linocut on paper, 170 × 620 cm
Purchased in 2020. G 13990

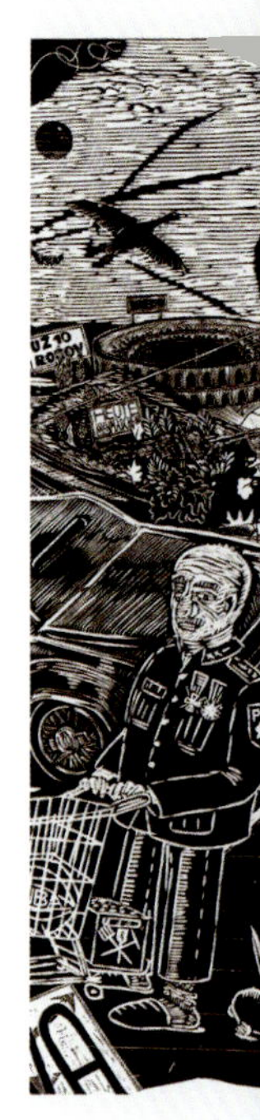

The large-scale print is permanently installed in the Slovak National Gallery; it forms part of the collection *Art in the Public Space.* The display references the old–new practice of locating art in public buildings. It is an element of a programme aimed at exploring the architecture of our premises, encouraging visitors to the gallery even if they do not visit an exhibition. A collective of authors and friends worked on the graphic artwork for three years: 'I called the guys to get together for carving. We smoked, read, sat on the floor and took turns at engraving.'

The impetus was the rise in popularity of conspiracy theories in our country. The main motif of the work draws upon historical events, cultural history, conspiracy theories and dialogue with graphic, literary and philosophical traditions. The connection is the fictional Fellowship of the Pentode, an order that controls the world from afar. Based on the engraving, the artists created a series of exceptional books that are a precise 1:1 scale map of the work.

The publication *In the Name of the Pentode* achieved first place in the bibliophilia category in the competition *Most Beautiful Czech Books 2018*. It provides the only key to the work ever published by the authors:

'Not everything is as it seems. There are visible forces in the world, but there are also invisible ones. The ability to read the signs and understand the connections is an essential prerequisite to understanding reality.'

This allows us to hope that perhaps the stupidity may be ironic.

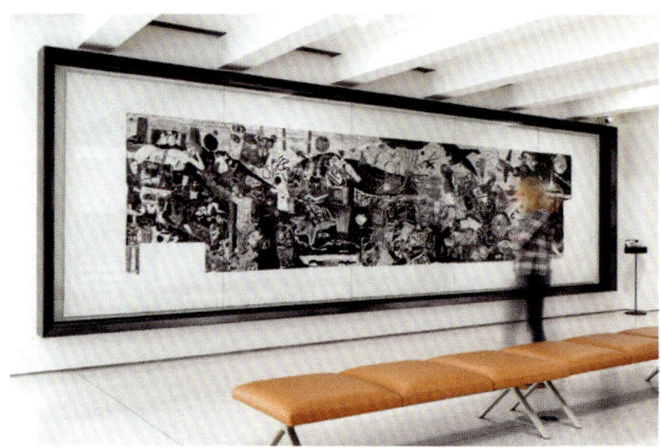

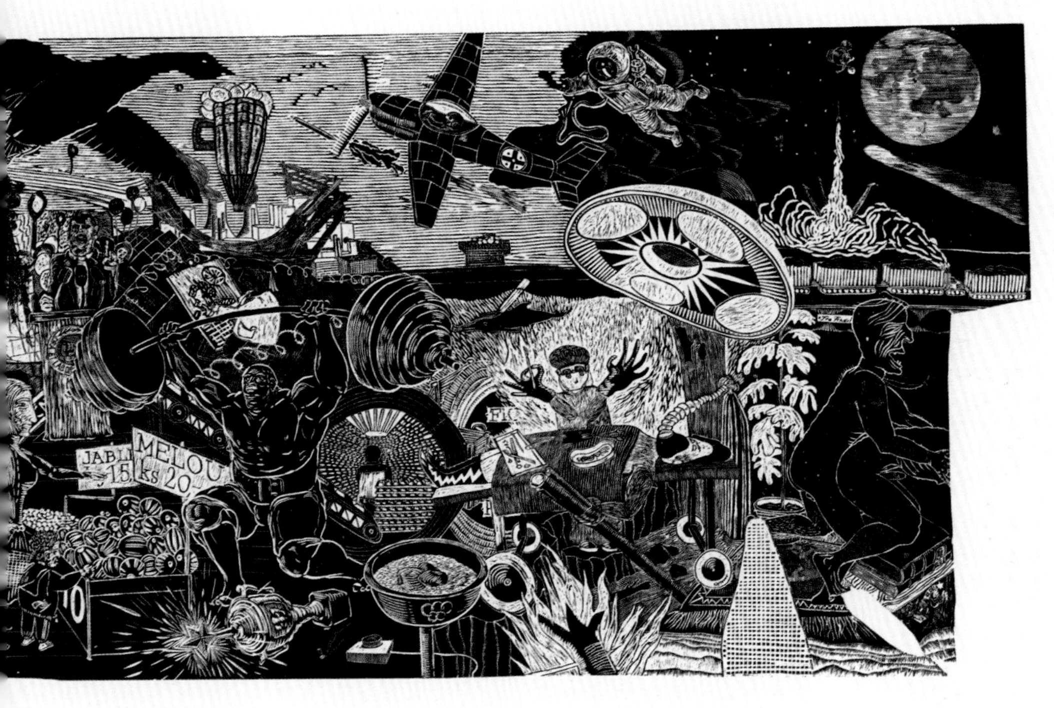

JABI
MELOU
15
ks 20

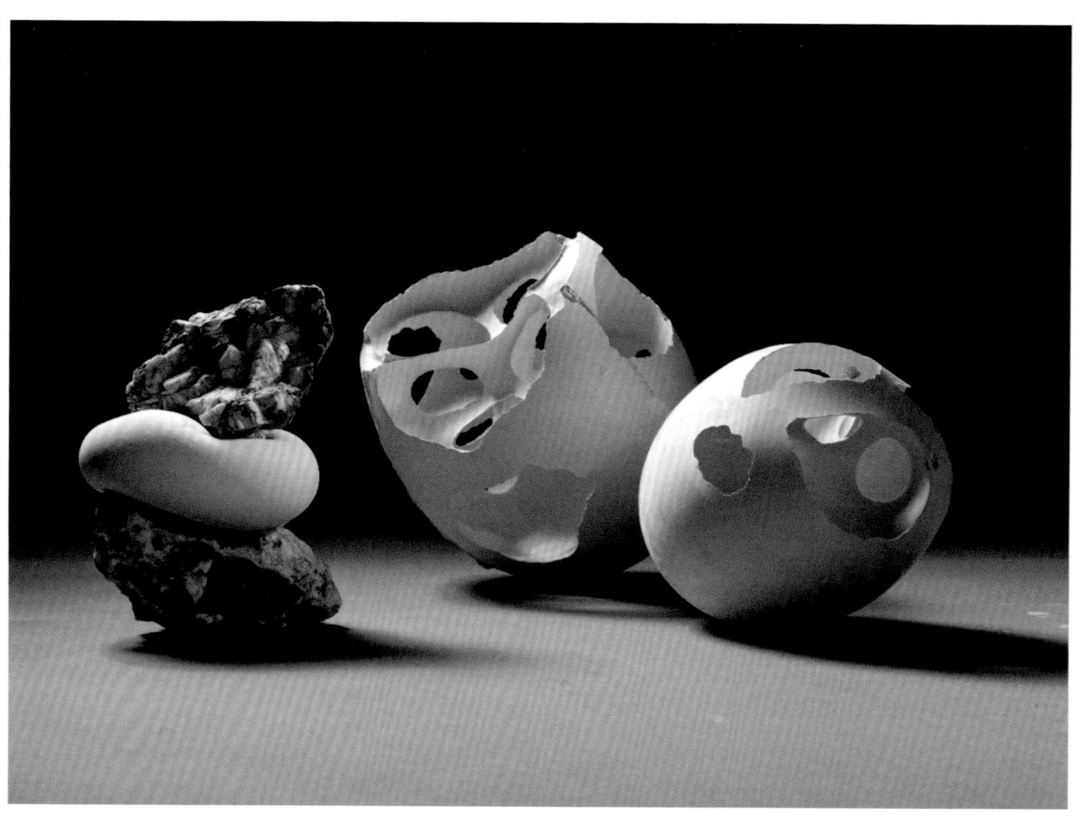

MARIA BARTUSZOVÁ (1936–1996)

Untitled. 1985–87

Plaster cast, stones, 30 × 15 cm; 29 × 28 × 25.5 cm; 19 × 24.5 × 19 cm

Purchased in 2000. P 2657, P 2659, P 2660

Today Maria Bartuszová is not only one of our most appreciated sculptors of the second half of the twentieth century, but generally the most appreciated sculptor in all Slovak art. This was confirmed by her retrospective at the Tate Modern gallery in London (2022). Part of the story is also the 'legend' of her relocation from Prague to Košice, where she continually worked in the shadow of her husband, also a sculptor. Although Bartuszová operated in both architecture and exteriors, her most prized works are her fragile plaster objects. She had an outright fascination with the material magic of plaster – initially a substance of powder, a loose mass, but one that when combined with water transformed into a fluid substance capable of transformations and rapid yet economically accessible experiments.

Such properties enabled Bartuszová to take an innovative approach to the material and the process of gradual solidification. She utilised rubber moulds, combinations of natural materials and various explorations of casting and moulding. By focusing on experimentation, and combining and layering techniques in various ways, she reached a level of skill that makes it difficult to discern how some of her works were created. Today we can interpret her work in relation to ecofeminism in its latent and intuitive version: that of a natural path in which the central category is nature, cyclical processes, interconnectedness, capacity for transformation and dynamism, in conjunction with the inner and fundamental or primordial energy.

Bartuszová's work was the subject of our first retrospective at the Slovak National Gallery (2005), when we transferred almost her entire studio to the exhibition space. That experience resonates with me to this day, all the more because current presentations of her work are much cleaner and more minimalist.

EMÍLIA RIGOVÁ (born 1980)

Vomite ergo sum! 2018
Digital video recording, 45 sec.
Purchased in 2019. IM 1024

The curator chose this recent acquisition as an example of the
work of an artist who intelligently tackles Roma themes but is
not primarily an activist; she rather stays within the boundaries
of contemporary art. In this respect, the work is a breakthrough
for our collections. We have many that focus on the picturesque
or problematic nature of Roma culture, but that do not go beyond
the level of observation. Although the work of the artist – Emília
Rigová aka Bári Raklóri – cannot be reduced to themes of (her)
Roma identity, she has worked mostly in this area in recent years.
It is here that she has had the most interesting results.

Rigová succeeds in capturing what most fascinates and simultaneously unsettles some people about the Roma ethnic group. Her
simple video works on multiple levels – drawing on traditions of the
Roma community, but also on a universal phenomenon. In a loop,
the artist, dressed in black and on all fours, vomits liquid gold – the
status symbol of financially secure Roma. Roma women's habit of
retaining their possessions as jewellery, which they always carry
with them so as not to be left empty-handed if they are rejected by
their husbands (or by the community), also plays a role. Gold is thus
not only a reflection of status, but also a statement of security for the
future. The gesture is – like the bulimic stumble – a testimony to the
ambivalence of self-acceptance, an expulsion of something that is
an essential part of her and to which she continually returns. This
work is a personal, rather intimate and theatrical testimony which
at the same time achieves an extraordinary general scope.

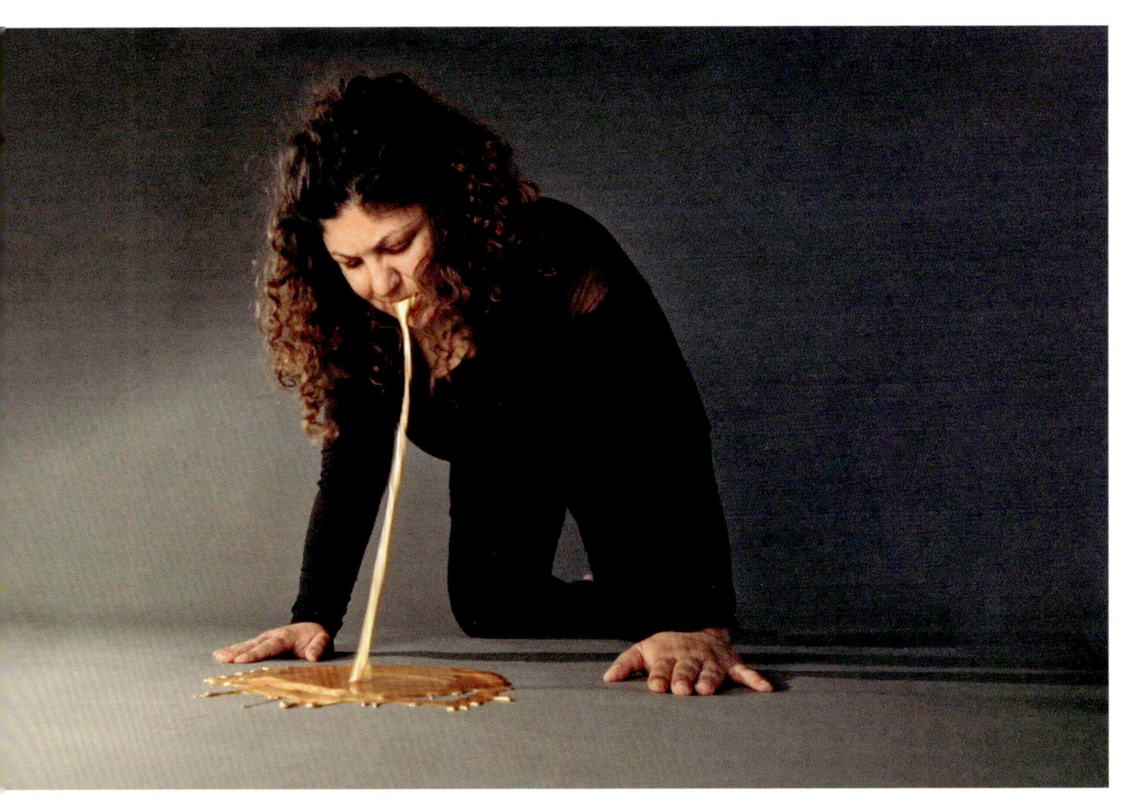

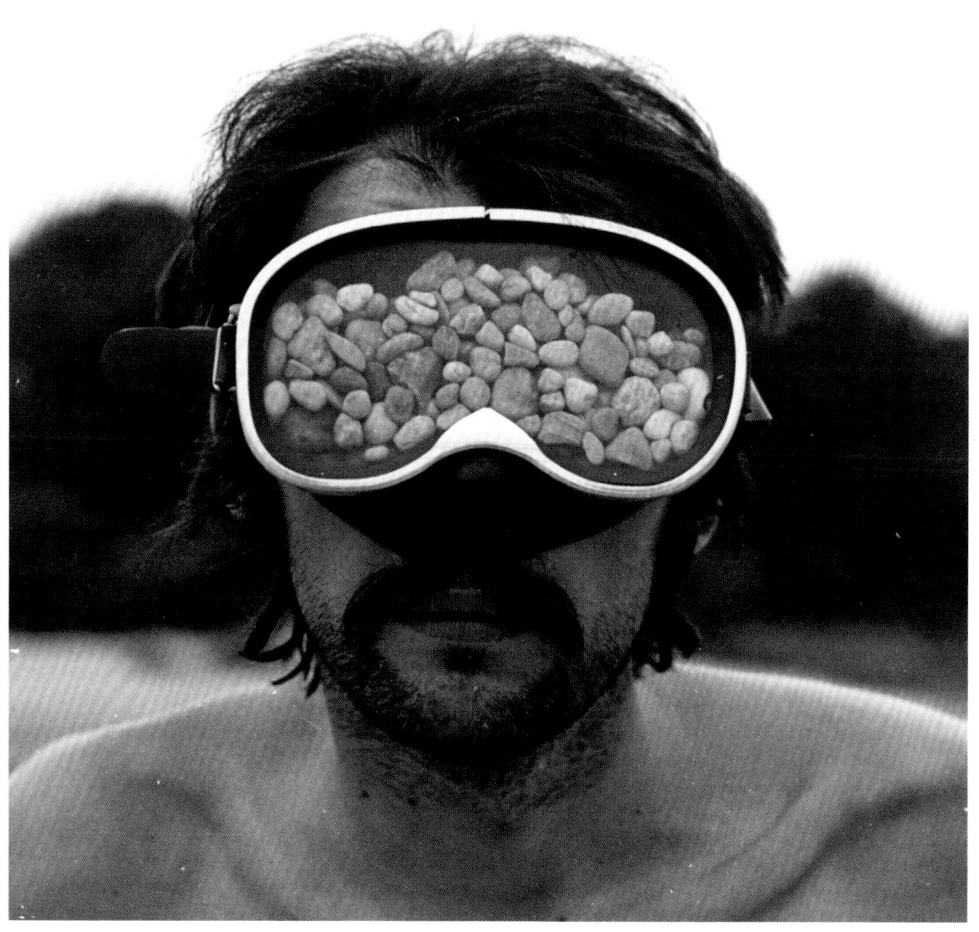

ĽUBOMÍR ĎURČEK (born 1948)

Self-portrait with Diver's Goggles. 1978

Positive on photographic paper, 22.8 × 20.7 cm

Purchased in 2003. IM 72

The artist was part of the alternative scene of the 1970s. He was among those who organised and participated in art happenings and events, but was never one of its loud and outspoken representatives. Ďurček was consistent, always precise and economical in his artistic expression, as typified by the black and white photography he used as a recording medium. He often reported critically and bluntly on contemporary times – for example, through an event in which he rang a friend's doorbell then, when the friend opened the door, stood there with a newspaper stuffed in his mouth, displaying a rallying slogan. Ďurček waited until the friend comprehended the situation, then left without a word. The action must have been confusing at the time, even frightening to some.

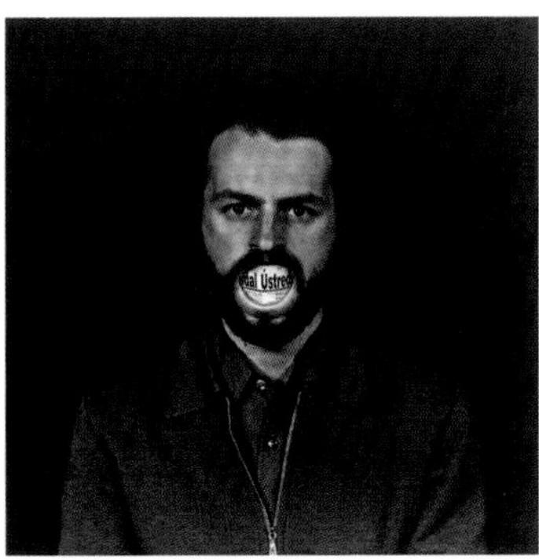

ĽUBOMÍR ĎURČEK: *Visitor.* 1980. Black and white positive on photographic paper, 28 × 28 cm. Purchased in 1990. IM 40

We hold it in our collections, but I chose instead this self-portrait, part of a wider series created to document the actions of Ďurček and his friends. They went together to a popular natural bathing spot, a lake near Bratislava, where the artists created temporary works from found materials. This photograph is probably the most powerful taken at the time; we used it on a large billboard on our gallery frontage. The artist piled stones into his diving goggles. Did he no longer want to, or was he no longer able to, look at what was going on around him? Did he place the stones there so as not to emerge again? Or was he simply illustrating a figure of speech about having dust thrown into one's eyes?

JOZEF SUŠIENKA (born 1937)

Park Sculpture. 1970–74

Glazed clay and stoneware, variable dimensions
Purchased in 2019. UP-DK 5400

The work of the ceramist and sculptor Jozef Sušienka is a powerful example within twentieth-century Slovak art of the empathic
interplay of environment, ceramic sculpture and man. The artist
has been cultivating this theme since the 1960s, long before ecology
became a global challenge and a necessity of life. In this medita-
tive, Zen-energy-laden play, ovoid and other organic shapes act as
portents of contextually unfolding environmental realisations. His
Boulders, *Shells*, *Puffballs*, *Creatures* and *Martians* rarely remain
solitary; their strength is in growing, multiplying, grouping. They
can be an introverted assemblage, inconspicuously dispersed into
the natural or urban environment, or bold, imposing verticals in
which Sušienka multiplies an identically shaped module in an
open, variable combinations.

    Sušienka's works are eminently recognisable due to his persis-
tent research into surface structures using sculptural, painterly and
graphic means – from glazes to incisions, decals and perforations.
He is one of few Slovak ceramists who defined themselves against
the then communist glorification of the potter's wheel. He prefers
to experiment with raw factory blanks, from which he almost literally 'knocks out' the shape using his particular authorial method.
Sušienka did not become any type of 'utilitarian'; he is a sculptor in
ceramics. We can add that we certainly wish to share the author's
hope that the forces and processes of nature are in our favour. This
is why a series of 'mushrooms' is a permanent feature in the courtyard of the Slovak National Gallery.

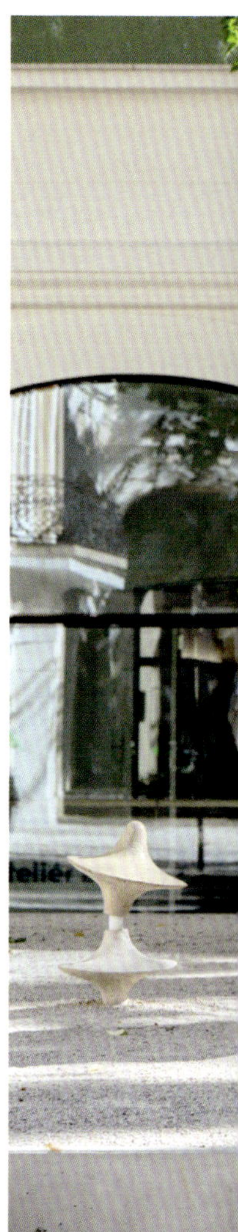

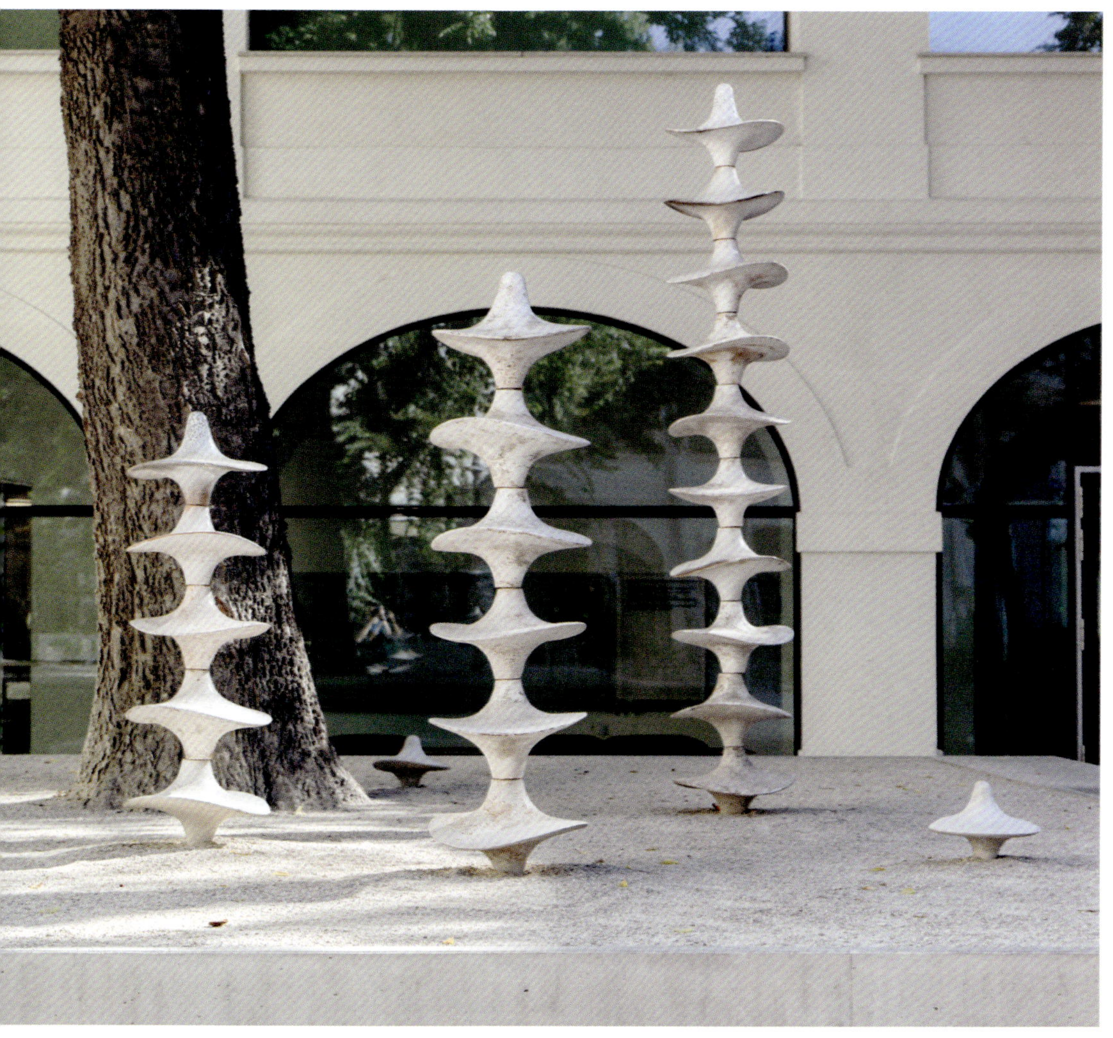

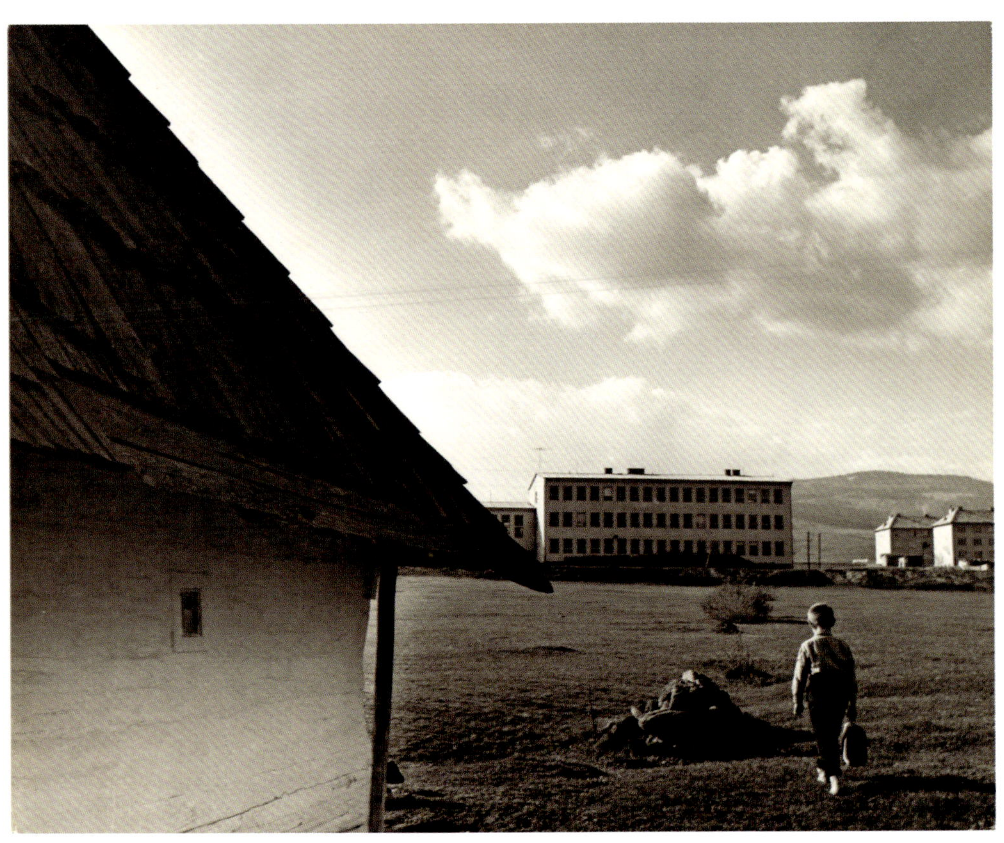

KAROL KÁLLAY (1926–2012)

To the School. 1958

Black and white photograph, photographic paper, pasteboard, 49 × 59.1 cm

Purchased in 1961. UP-DK 45

This artist is one of the most important photographers of the second half of the twentieth century across a wide range of subjects, partly because he had the rare opportunity to travel abroad during the communist period. This civilian image has a typical cultural and social, even propagandistic background, but the effect transcends it many times over. The lives and portraits of children have been a frequent subject for photographers, especially for amateur ones. During the period of socialist development they became a popular topic – besides natural photographic interest, there was an important, even state-forming impulse. Photographers often portrayed children and young people in general because they were about to experience communism. In fact, they became a living symbol of communist eschatology.

There was thus a rare harmony between ideological demands and natural human interest. Countless images were commissioned depicting, in various forms, the state's care of children. New school buildings were being built for them – in Karol Kállay's well-known photograph, a young schoolboy walks directly from a wooden cottage in the foreground towards a new school, constructed in typical rough functionalist style. A spectacular, symbolic image of the new conditions was created.

The underlying message is much more profound, however. The shot is neither jubilant nor happy, as art of the time was expected to be. Instead it appeals with a form of timeless, melancholic beauty – the boy is in an interspace, caught between the old and the new. He may be embracing the new, but the nostalgia and beauty of the old is by no means a discarded dimension.

JOZEF JANKOVIČ (1937–2017)

Spiderweb. 1969

Polychrome polyester, metal, rope, 212 × 103 × 103 cm

Purchased in 1989. P 2501

Jozef Jankovič was a key figure of post-war sculpture and a pillar of artistic life. In terms of creation, he is a sculptor-figuralist, but one of a special type. The key theme of his work is humanity, whom he understood to be part of the history of manipulated beings. He views them with an ironic gaze, sometimes sarcastic or tragicomic.

Already before the mid-1960s, Jankovič began iconoclastically to polemicise with the official doctrine of socialist-realist sculpture, as well as with the idea of European anthropocentrism. He abandoned the traditional integrity of sculpture and, in an unprecedented manner, demonstrated the disintegration of the old wholeness of body and soul into horrifying elements of human substance. Perhaps the most characteristic element of Jankovič's work is the way in which he deals with the category of corporeality, present in a deformed state within his works. From his early works onwards, Jankovič broke the human body into fragments and traces: amorphous limbs, moving arms and legs. He acquired their characteristic indeterminate and vaguely swollen shape somewhat by chance, pouring malleable plaster experimentally into stocking and glove moulds. Later he elevated this element to the central motif of his work.

Spiderweb is the prototype of this strange, Jankovič-esque creature of the 1960s. It emerges as a confluence of moving parts: sagging, biomorphic protuberances, limp dangling legs and protruding arms, all enclosed in a cage, confined, entangled in nets and spiders' webs. They reveal, often too directly and cruelly, the contrasting sides of human power and powerlessness. It was for this straightforward humanist appeal that Jankovič was persecuted by the then socialist regime. Complementing the architecture of the building, two of his sculptures are permanently installed in our gallery.

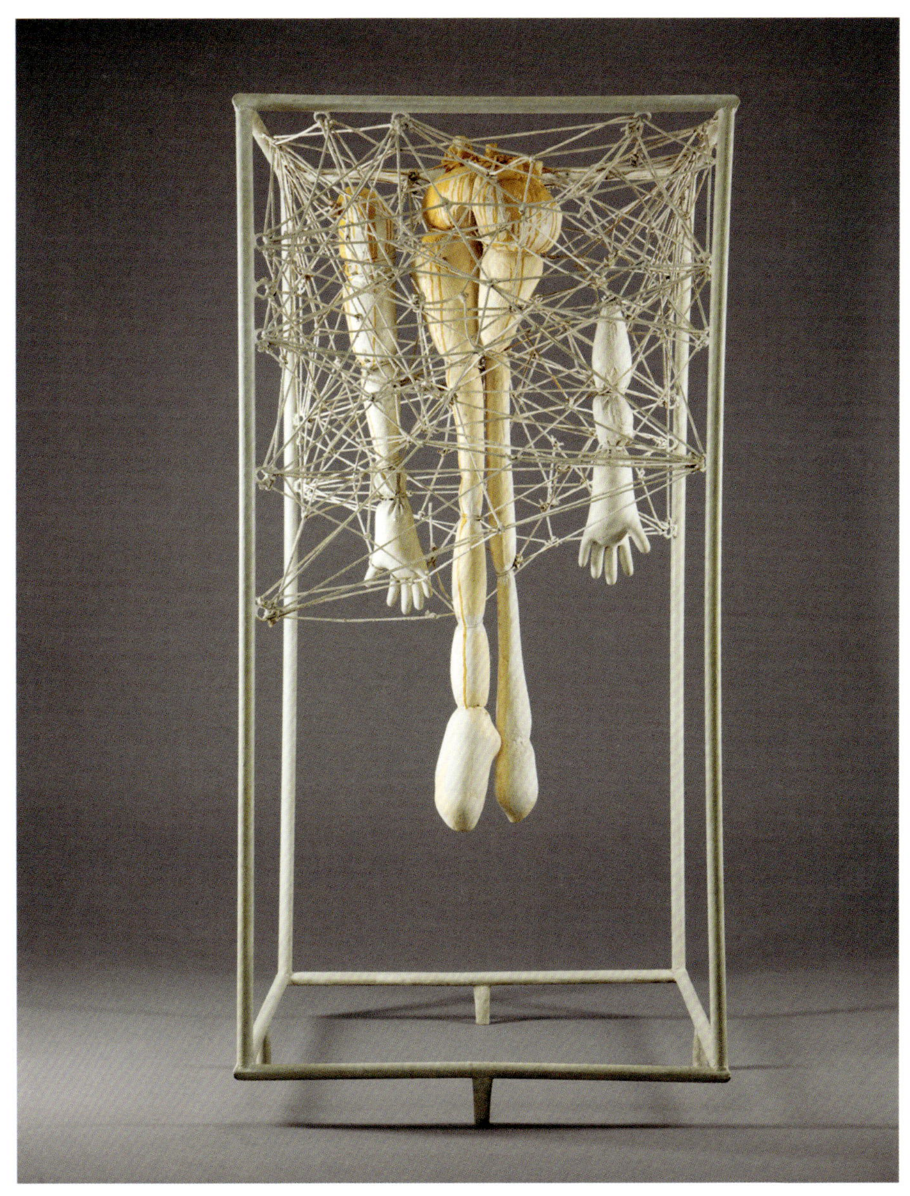

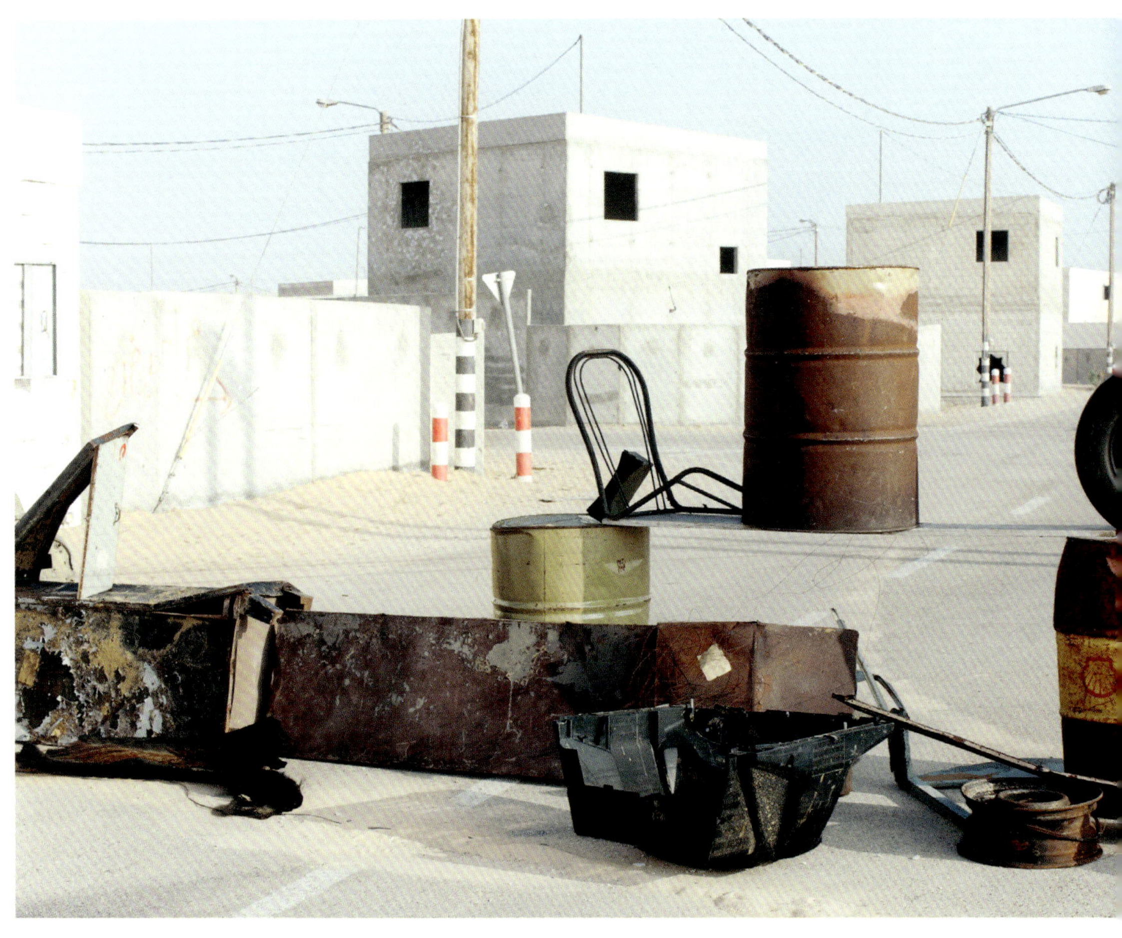

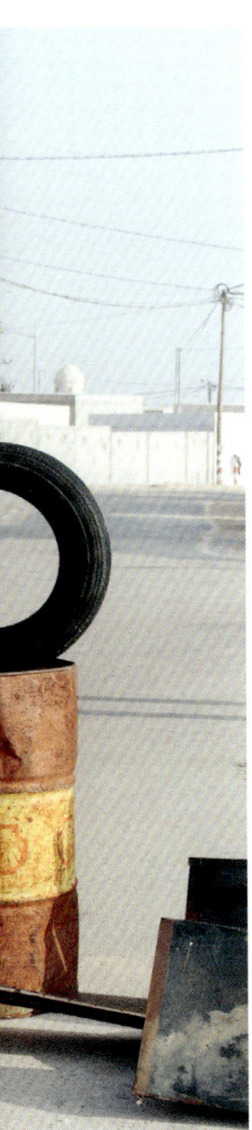

MARTIN KOLLAR (1971)

Field Trip. Israel. 2009–11

Colour photograph on RC photographic paper, 95 × 130 cm

Purchased in 2015. UP-DK 4807

The artist, one of the most outstanding photographers of his generation, has continued to shine from the 1990s onwards. Since then Kollar has confirmed his position on the scene, his importance long having outgrown Slovakia's borders, and he is now better known and more active in exhibitions abroad than at home. In addition to photography, Kollar is a successful film director. Although he works with found reality and does not manipulate photographs, he often chooses peculiar situations, unusual spaces, abandoned facilities and strange environments. Frequent subjects are 'transitional assemblages' – found situations that resemble carefully constructed installations. Their visual impact is amplified not only by being free of purposeful function, but also by containing an element of mystery. Often enigmatic, these softly suggestive clusters of objects refer to the core of a form of ever-present, eternal proto-surrealism – the surrealism contained in reality itself, as the well-known thesis of the surrealists contends.

However, that alone would not be enough. In the visual art of the past few decades, we can find many allusions to this surrealist primordial foundation. Over time, however, Martin Kollar increasingly heightens the tension between the attractively bizarre subject matter and its unobtrusively mundane presentation – as if the surrealist foundation were grafted with a style of conceptualised new materiality, a hallmark of the Düsseldorf school of photography. *Field Trip* belongs to this series. A somewhat cheerful barricade of junk items, tyres and oil drums can therefore also be read as a 'photograph of a levitating barrel'. The photograph became the cover for his exhibition and monograph in our gallery in 2015.

DENISA LEHOCKÁ (born 1971)

Untitled. 2023

Textile, embroidery, plaster, coins and potatoes, 15 × 2.75 m
The work is part of the Slovak National Gallery's architecture thanks
to a Tatra Banka donation to the public.

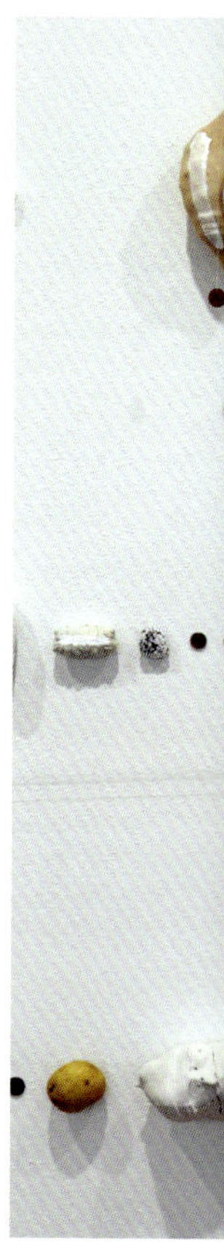

The monumental wall forms part of the architecture of the new Slovak National Gallery, conceptually representing a return to the pre-revolutionary (1989) practice of placing artworks in public institutions. We chose a work of contemporary art to convey subliminally somewhat complicated content to the visitor in a clearer way – presenting the vitality of contemporary art. The artist worked on the wall for more than a year and the result is a spatial collage. Yet it also forms a visual text, a musical score, visual poetry, an artistic landscape. The work offers viewers a chance to tune in, to appreciate singularities of the whole act and to find a voice that speaks to them personally.

The artist tries accurately to articulate the world around her and us. She uses 'ordinary' materials and techniques – plaster, natural materials, coins, casts and textile objects. She embroiders, shapes, combines and spins them, listening to the inner tension and then tuning everything together so that the objects find their exact and proper place. For the Slovak National Gallery, her work is also an attempt to say something essential about the nation that avoids reference to folklore tradition. That is why Lehocká uses only coins with an image of Mount Kriváň; that is why live potatoes are part of the installation; that is why small embroidered objects are literally 'huddled together' in stockings, resembling the scarved women in paintings and photos of the 'departing world'. As a result, the wall works as a landscape. You can sit in front of it for a long time, immersing yourself in it layer by layer.

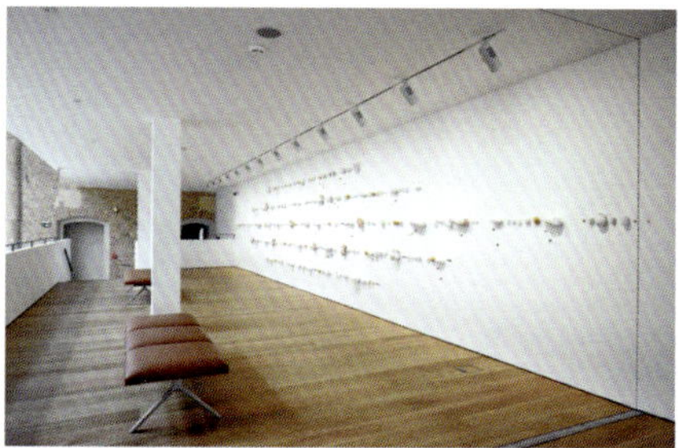

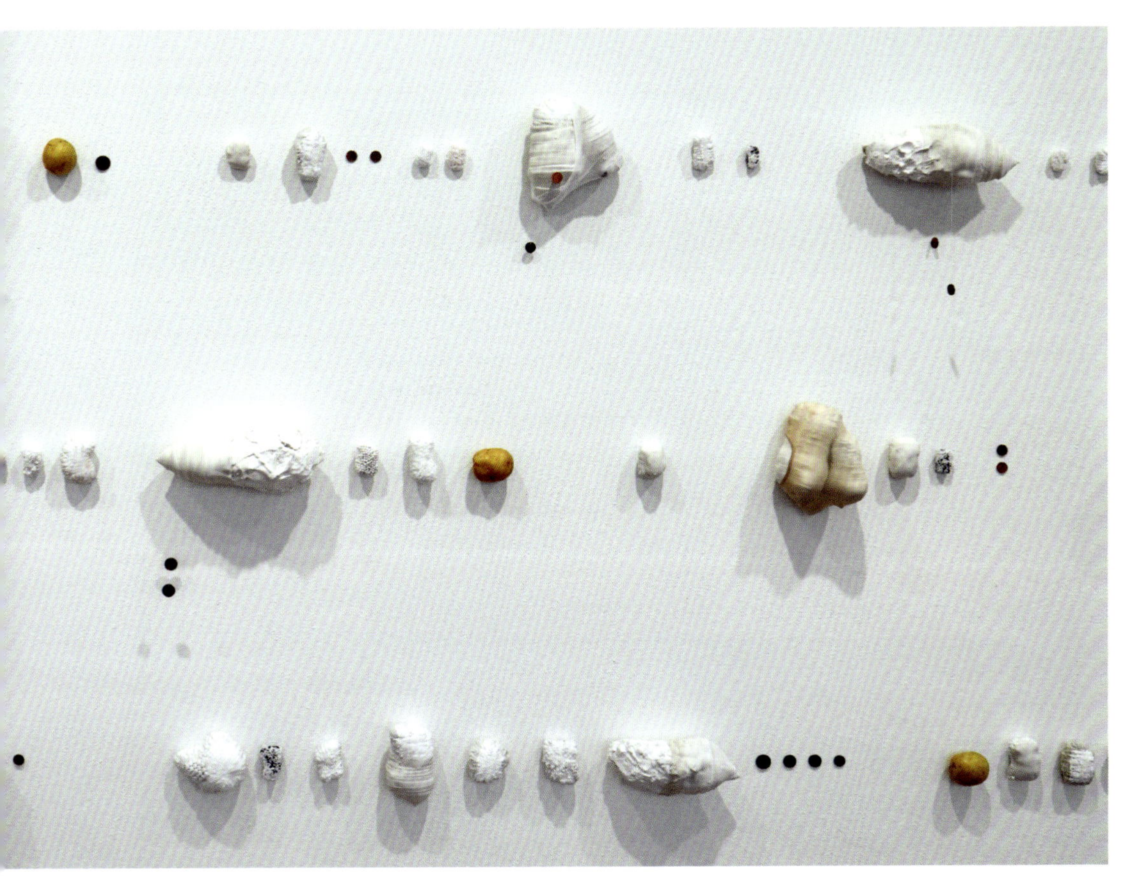

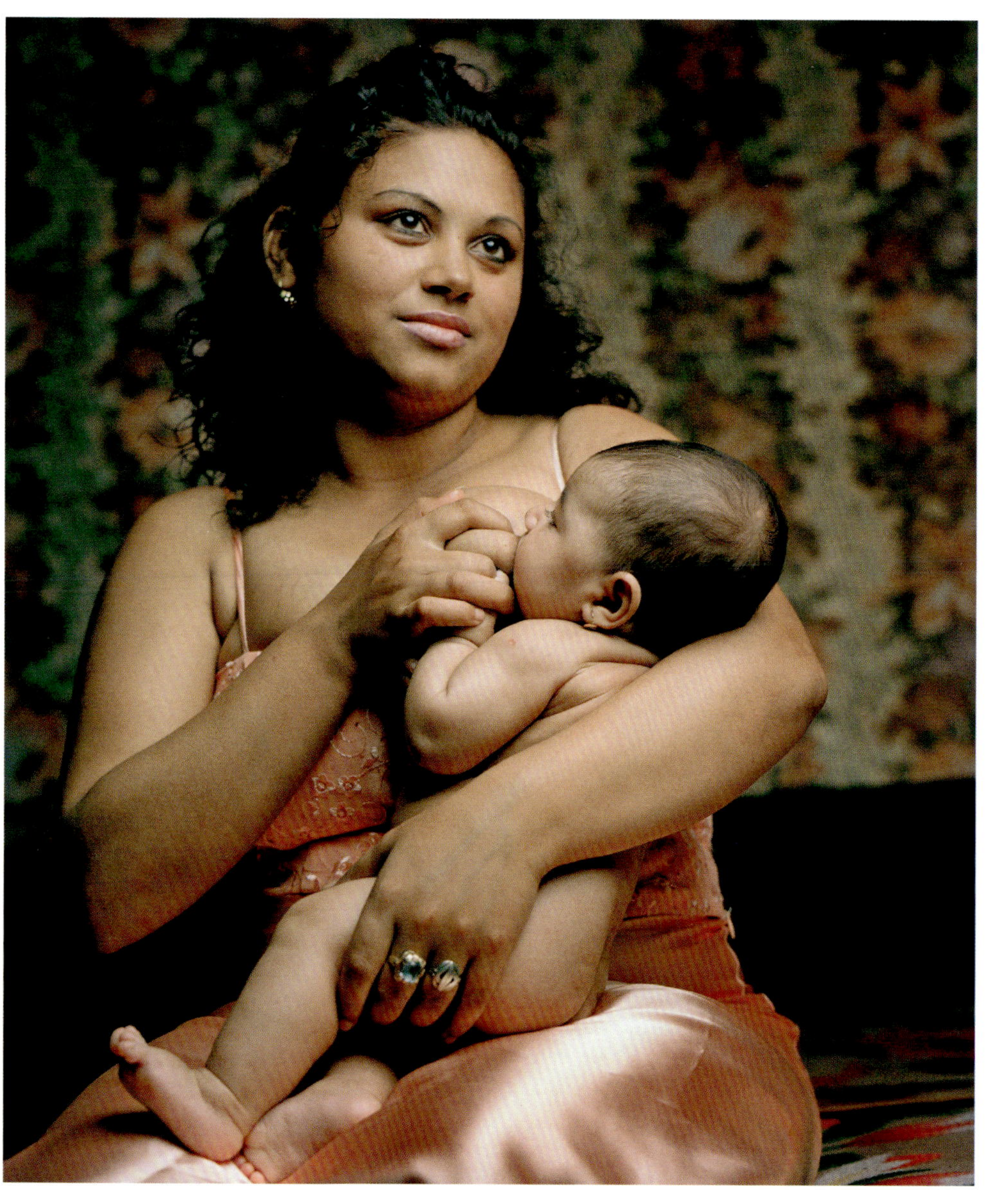

ŠYMON KLIMAN (born 1980)

Beautiful People. Jitka Pištová. 2008

Digital print on paper, 126.5 × 106.5 cm

Purchased in 2016. UP-DK 5178

Šymon Kliman's extensive and as yet unfinished photographic series *Beautiful People* is dedicated to documenting the Roma community. It was a popular genre in Slovakia during the 1980s because this was one of the last communities with a distinct visual identity, usually perceived as almost exotic. Kliman's photographs consciously and vigorously disrupt this established canon, clearly departing from the usual 'documentary' images of people living in Roma settlements.

Unlike his predecessors such as Josef Koudelka and Tibor Huszár, Kliman does not seek to follow the tradition of harsh, neo-romantically dark pictures of this environment. He does not emphasise those aspects of Roma life that are difficult for the Gorgios (the Roma term for the settled community) to understand. Instead he does exactly the opposite. Instead of the characteristic black-and-white photography, Kliman records 'vivid life' – a distinctive spectrum of colours in enlargements of grand, even pictorial formats. He does not seek to 'catch' his objects in their real environment. On the contrary, Kliman creates staged, almost studio portraits of individuals and couples, allowing them to present themselves as they wish to be seen. He uses the cliché of studio photography to confront another cliché – conventional notions of Roma life.

The resulting images are not only more colourful but also, contrary to popular conception, more optimistic and forward-looking. The documentary faithfulness is not lost, but is simply not pushed to the foreground. It remains preserved in details of the interiors, the real living environment of these people, which has only temporarily become the environment of the photographic studio. I chose them for this selection because of their interplay with an established post-colonial cliché.

STANISLAV FILKO (1937–2015)
FRANZ ANTON PALKO (1717–1766)

Grandpa – Grandma Listen to the Radio & Portrait of Empress Maria Theresa. 1965/1775–76

Found object, readymade, variable dimensions, assemblage/oil on canvas

Acquired as a gift in 2018. P 2868, O 7154

It was the decision of the curator Alexandra Homoľová to combine Filko's work with the imperial portrait from the collection display, one of many donated works from the Linea Collection. Since the Slovak National Gallery was established relatively recently, it was not founded on any large aristocratic, ecclesiastical or other donation. This deficiency was resolved a few years ago when a major collecting family donated to the national gallery a substantial collection of 150 works, all crucially linked to our environment and which we were able to select ourselves. A permanent display of these works is part of the agreement. Over time, the collectors began purposefully to build the collection, intending that it should be more than a mere repository of capital – it should support the telling and retelling of the story of Slovak art. The relationship between the institution and the patrons did not end with the display; we continue to add further works to the collection through donations.

Filko's object is temporally related to the famous *Altars to Contemporaneity* series from the 1960s. In contrast to their universal messages, however, it bears a personal significance related to the artist's childhood memories. The portrait of the Empress is literally unique in our collections (not to mention in art), as we do not hold representative portraits at all. It is the juxtaposition of Filko and Palko that is significant, both for the content of the gift and for our perception of the cultural context. Bringing the two together is a beautiful crossing of time and an unexpectedly patriotic act, a way of gracefully tackling the imperial legacy.

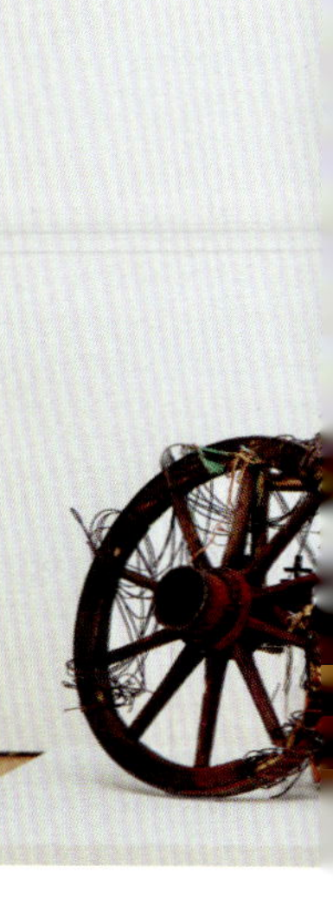

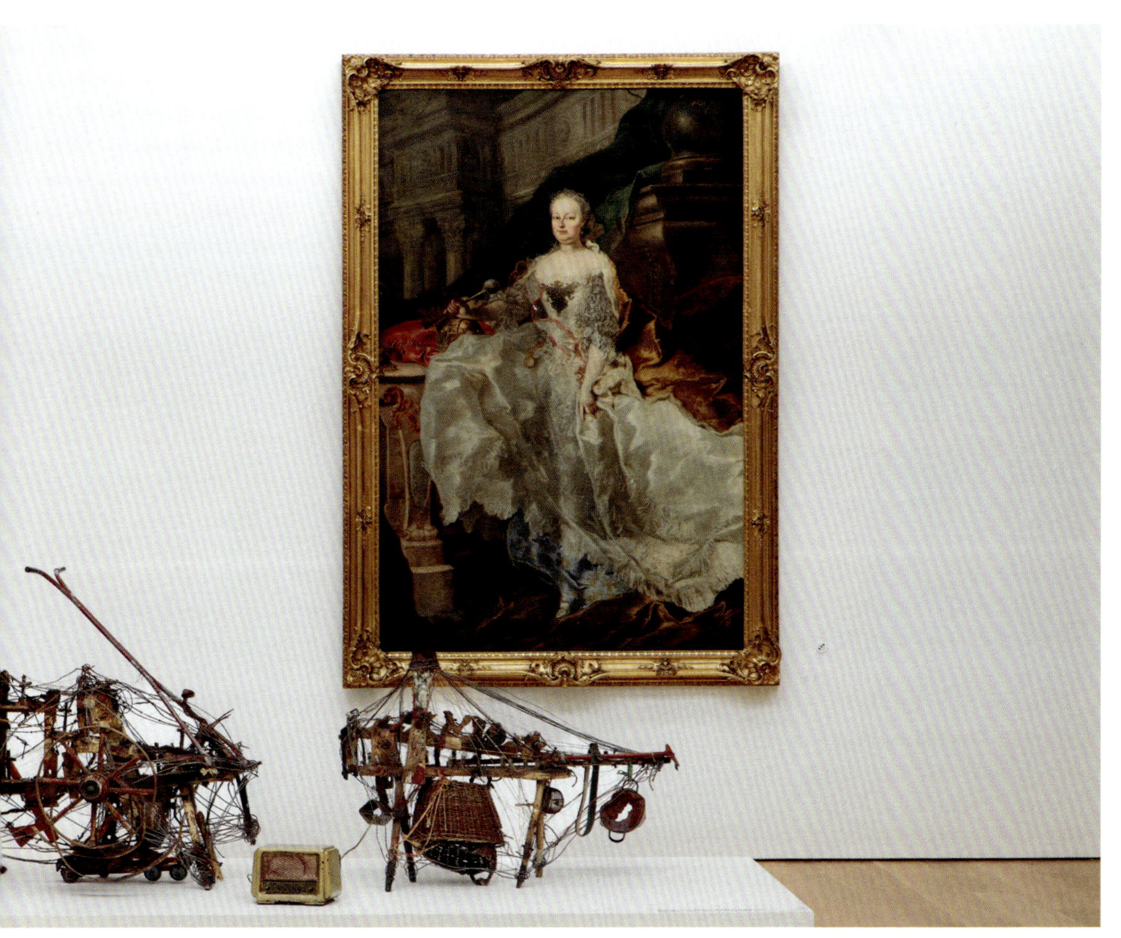

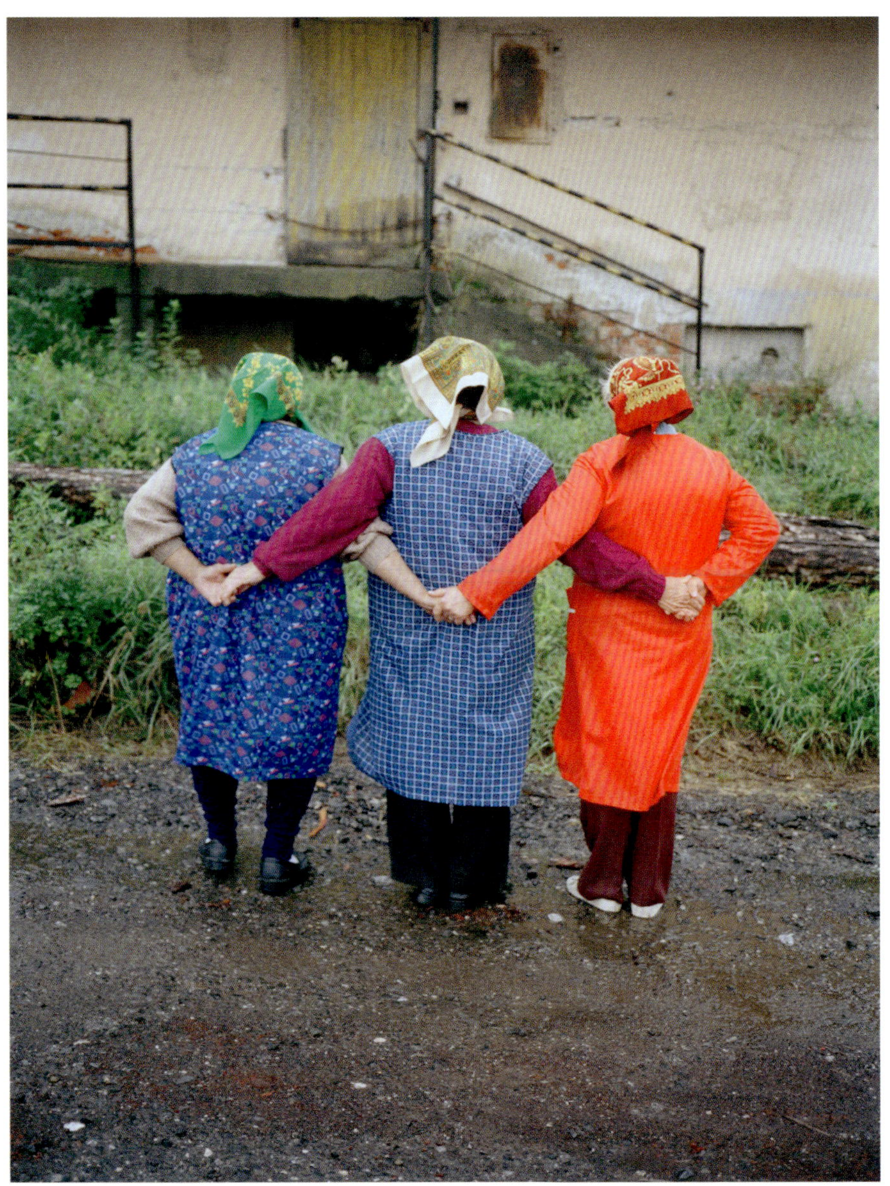

LUCIA NIMCOVÁ (born 1977)

Unofficial II. 2007

Colour digital print, 67.3 × 55.8 cm

Purchased in 2011. UP-DK 4204

Our gallery holds an extensive collection of photographs, one that began to be built up over the last few decades. The collection comprises more documentary than artistic works, reflecting the distribution of quality on the domestic scene. This trend survives in contemporary photography in the works of Martin Kollar and artists such as Lucia Nimcová, a photographer, researcher and curator who engages in 'photographic research of society' and creates the series 'in the making', which is continually reconfigured, variously becoming a book, a curated exhibition or an internet project.

Although she lives in the west of the country, Nimcová works with the east. Her major theme is Humenné (a town in the far east of Slovakia) – its people, environments, family histories and collective memory. These are generally solitary images, situationally motivated or based on photographs of older colleagues. They exude ostalgia as well as an eastern rusticity. This living space fascinates Nimcová. She seeks to uncover and communicate its cultural and photographic potential. For this photographer, Humenné is still a form of navel of the world – a microcosm, in whose visual archaeology the socialist memory of the region and its current second life are revealed in a unique and yet typical way.

The socialist sediment permeates the images, both the environments and the human physiognomies. The fact that this is not a stylisation but a portrayal of how the east apparently is, and that only we 'Westerners' from Bratislava mistakenly believe this to be an 'ostalgia', is supported by another work of ours, a painting by Lucia Dovičáková. Also an artist from the east, she independently works with the very same motif.

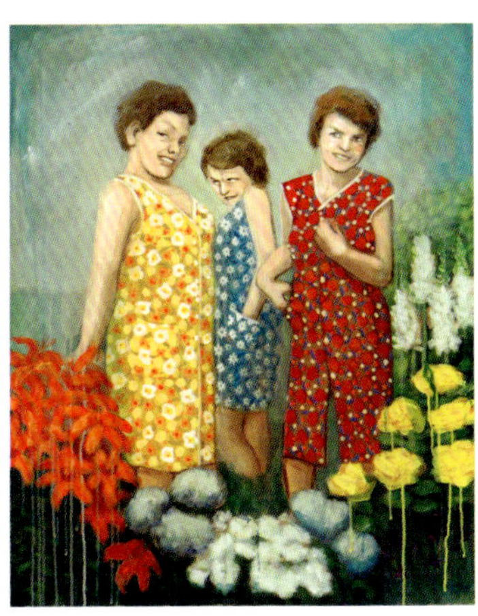

LUCIA DOVIČÁKOVÁ (born 1981): *Dress Apron* (2009). Acrylic on canvas. Purchased in 2012. O 6963

LADISLAV BIELIK (1939–1984)

August 1968. 1968

Black and white photograph on photographic paper, 27.5 × 38.2 cm

Purchased in 1990. UP-DK 1531/a, c, k

The artist was a sports photojournalist who tragically died rather young in the exercise of his profession. His series of images documenting the mood and atmosphere on the streets of Bratislava following the arrival of the Soviet occupation troops is unique, yet not typical of his output. The most famous image from a set of photographs taken during the first days after 21 August 1968 circulated throughout Slovak media; it has become a symbol of its time. Interestingly, this image was not attributed to the photographer, who preferred not to admit authorship publicly because it was detrimental to his work and social life. It was only attributed to Bielik after 1989. Almost immediately, the Slovak National Gallery's curator acquired it

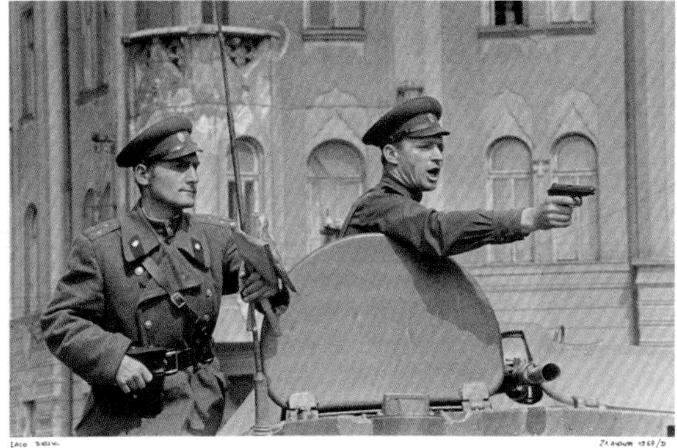

for our collections, along with a substantial body of the artist's works.

The image is part of a larger series reflecting the situation in Bratislava (especially in the square in front of the Arts and Law faculties of Comenius University). Some photographs show a strange mixture of despair and a preponderance of demonstrators. Others document brute foreign force, for example where a soldier stands in the turret of a tank and points a gun before him. These images are Slovakia's most significant photographic collection dedicated to these events. They are not the only material on the subject, however; within the Slovak National Gallery's collections we also have a photo series by Pavel Hudec-Ahasver and the diaries of Július Koller.

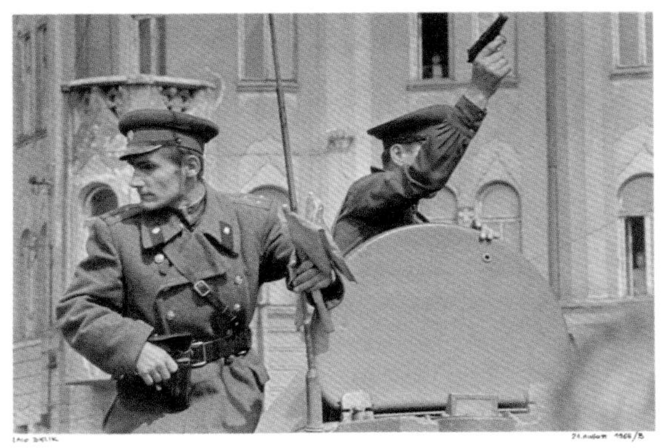

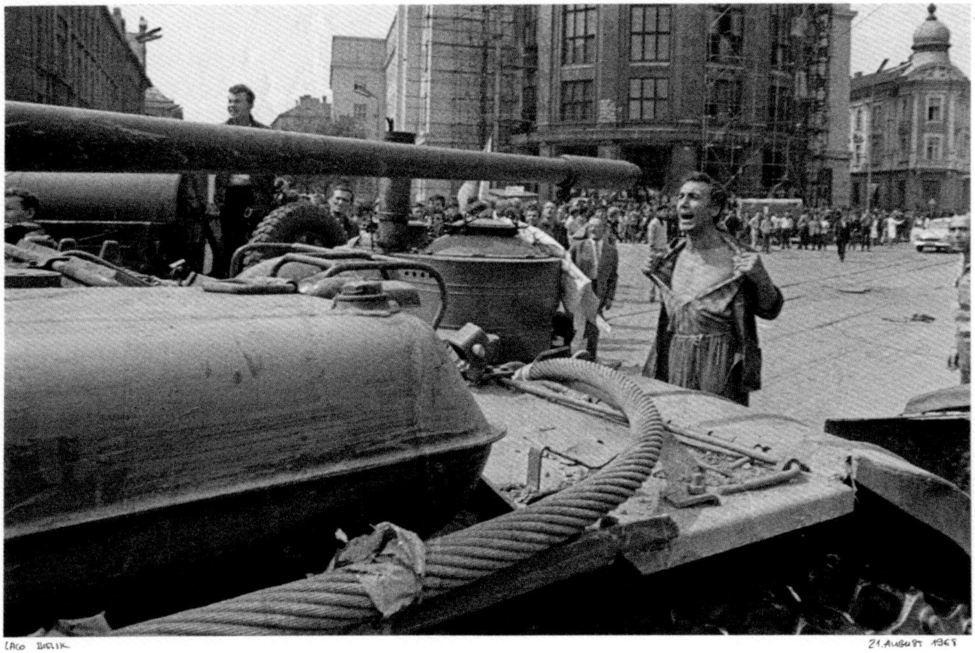

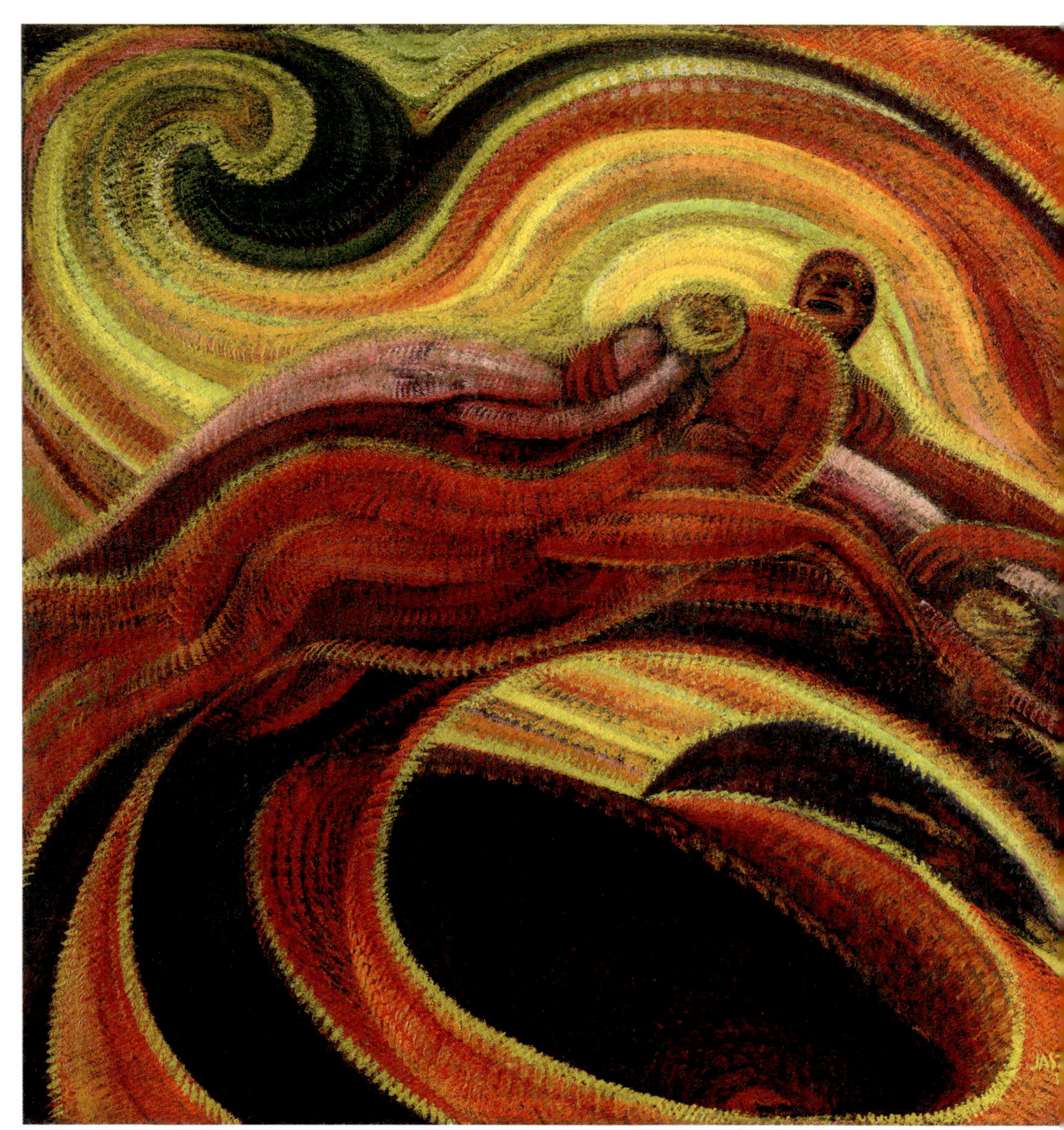

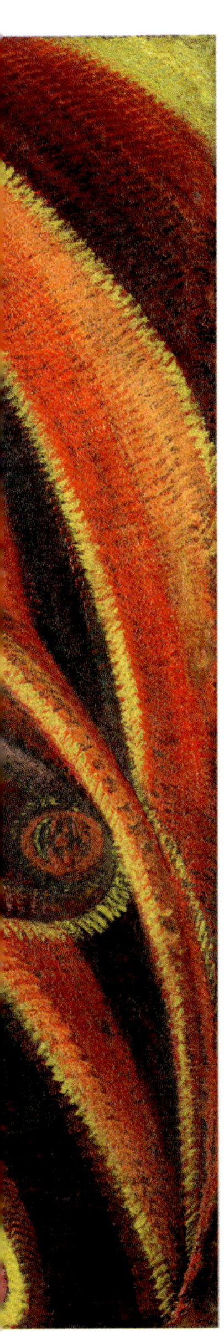

ANTON JASUSCH (1882–1965)

Might of the Sun. 1922–24

Oil on jute canvas, 149 × 172 cm

Acquired as a transfer in 2013. O 7007

Anton Jasusch is a somewhat unlikely phenomenon in Slovak art. His complicated life contributes to the romantic perception of his person and his work, complemented by the fact that most of his vast canvases burned down in a fire at the East Slovak Gallery in Košice (1985). His career as a painter was fatally disrupted by the First World War; he fought on the Russian front, then on the Italian front and in the famous battle of Piave, and then again on the Russian front, where he was taken prisoner. There followed Russian and Japanese prison camps, malarial fever and a harrowing journey through India, China, Korea and Malaya.

The experience changed Jasusch, marking him forever. Yet he capitalised on it in his painting – phantasmal images of exotic nature formed the framework of symbolic figurative scenes. It also left traces in the artist's sceptical, often mocking and ironic view of bourgeois lifestyle, morality and the banal values of his contemporaries. In this respect Jasusch is one of the most striking examples of the peripherality of Slovak Modern, of the peculiarities of its reaction to external stimuli.

Through a conjunction of circumstances that removed him from normal artistic life for a long period at a decisive moment in his artistic formation, providing him with only fragmentary and mediated sources of inspiration, but also through his compulsive need to express the most personal, unrepeatable feelings and opinions, Jasusch created in a few years of artistic preoccupation a work that will probably forever stand out from the dogmatic models of modernism – both domestic and European.

ANNA DAUČÍKOVÁ (born 1950)

Upbringing by Touch I. 1996
Black and white photograph, 39.8 × 37 cm
Purchased in 2017. IM 916/1

At the Slovak National Gallery we began working more closely with this artist in 2016 when preparing the first comprehensive publication for her exhibition at the documenta in Kassel (2017) – followed a few years later by her first professional exhibition (2019). The arrangements showed how wide the scope of her work is; from being a glassmaker, jeweller and painter, Anna Daučíková also became a photographer, video performer and video artist, experimenting with artistic types, techniques and processes of creation. She even transformed herself; she transformed the experience of the 'own' and 'foreign' body into an experience and conceptualisation of a third sex and gender that transcends established understandings of both femininity and masculinity.

The biographical line of Daučíková's story is also interesting. She persistently and genuinely searched for her path and place – within both a physical body and a physical place – and emigrated several times, the most interesting experience being a multi-year emigration to the Soviet Union in the 1980s. She in fact lived between different fixed points for a long time. Daučíková addresses all these experiences and feelings in an intelligent, non-activist way in her work. Reading the biographical interview in her ensemble catalogue, the intertwining of life experience and art is evident. I could not decide whether to choose a representative painting with numbers or a shot from a video. Finally, I chose the video, precisely because she herself is performing there. It is she who directly offers the viewer her own experience, and there is something deeply personal yet transcending of the individual in that.

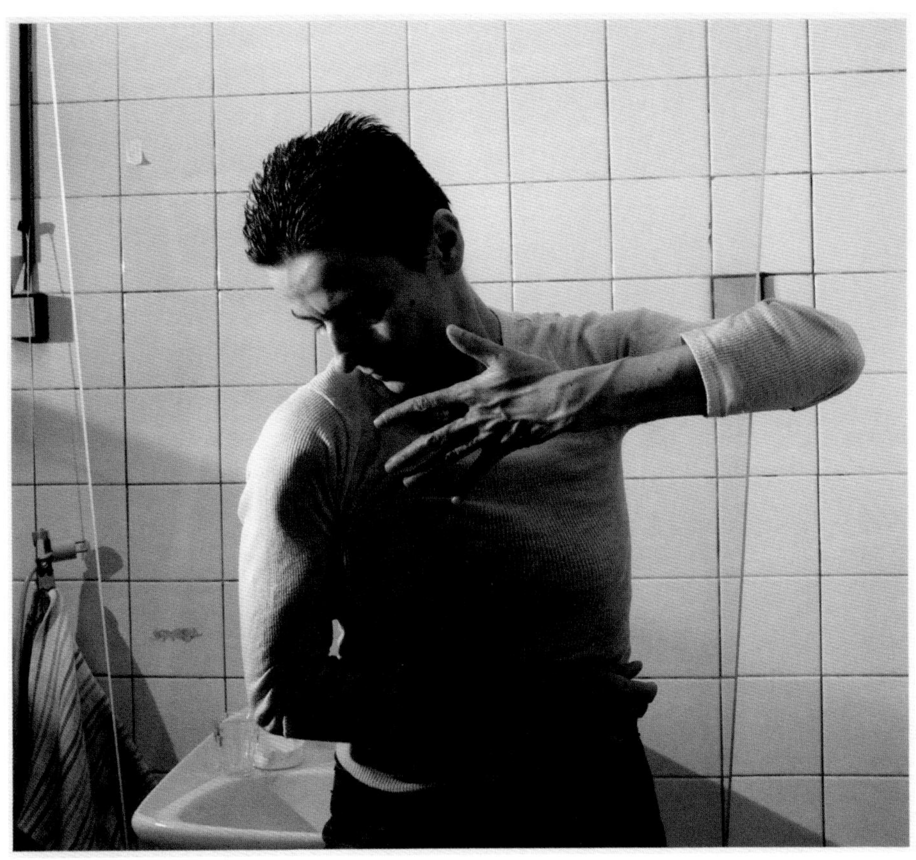

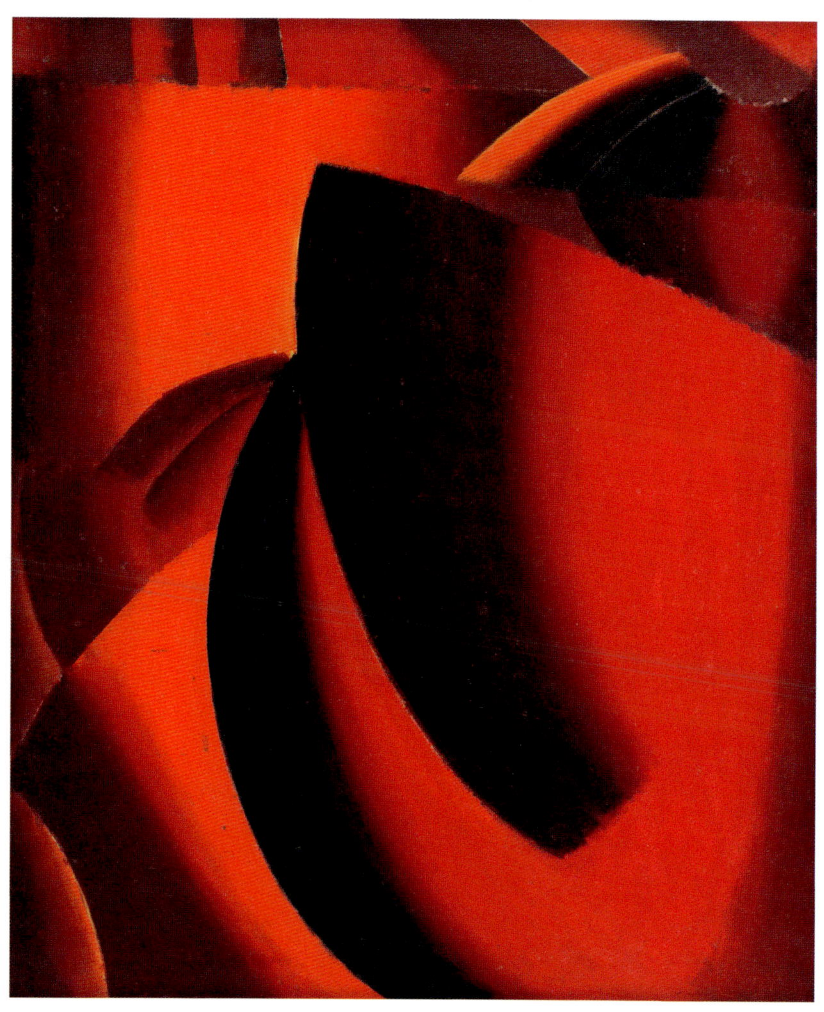

MILAN LALUHA (1930–2013)

Red Composition. 1966

Oil on canvas, 73 × 60 cm

Purchased in 1966. O 3183

Laluha belongs to the generation that entered the scene following the period of Stalinist socialist realism. He embraced a programme based on sincerity and inner authenticity of expression, the art of 'solid and simple shapes'. Within his work, he began programmatically to develop the principles of classical modernism and neomodern. Soon he discovered and implemented his own characteristic artistic formula, the eponymous Laluha formula of the image – a style he developed from cubo-futurist starting points. He builds the image from large square and rounded forms, drawn in an almost sculptural manner.

Simultaneously, however, Laluha enlivens the shapes with colour. Deploying a typically vibrant, almost fiery note, he then adds green and blue to red and yellow, accentuating them with contrasting black and white. Sometimes he chooses a soft colour scale, but at other times he reaches for darker tones; the result is a subdued twilight. Primarily he works with landscapes, often enriching them with figurative elements. Laluha frequently thematises the spiritual birthplace of his work, his native village in central Slovakia, the land of his childhood and youth that became his artistic destiny. With an extraordinary, almost hallucinatory obsession, he portrays the diverse faces of this world: the village in night- and daytime, trees and houses, still lifes, women and men, reapers and hay rakers. The result is an image that moves along a peculiar border between depicting and not depicting, traditional subject and unconventional modern form, the archaic and the innovative. The image serves as a curious visual fiction and a poetic metaphor at the same time. In this respect, this work is not typical Laluha, yet it carries something extra – the psychedelic aesthetic of the 1960s.

The Slovak National Gallery manages the richest collection of sacred art among the nation's public institutions. This is a result of cultural policy under communism; religious activities were suppressed, so art became the preferred domain for cult objects, which were transferred to museums and galleries. Other artefacts have been preserved in their original locations in churches, mostly in the custody of the Catholic Church. Since the Middle Ages, our art has been part of changing state formations (the Kingdom of Hungary, Austria-Hungary). The collection thus evinces a supra-regional character and the works on display reflect many international influences and impulses.

The turn of the sixteenth century, represented by most statues in the photograph opposite, can unhesitatingly be described as a 'golden age' for sacred art due to the mass production of altars, especially in northeastern regions of the country (Spiš, Šariš, Levoča, Košice). The economic boom and a favourable location at the crossroads of international trade routes led to the growth of cities that became attractive destinations for artists from influential centres such as Kraków, Nuremberg and Vienna. Moreover, thanks to the development of graphic templates, art was arguably becoming 'globalised' during this period. Consequently, for the first time in the history of art, some regions of Slovakia became not only part of important international artistic currents, but also a co-determiner of their quality. The Slovak National Gallery presents its rich holdings of Gothic and Baroque art in two long-term collection displays. The present photograph is from Bratislava, while a selection of other important artefacts can be seen at the medieval Zvolen Castle.

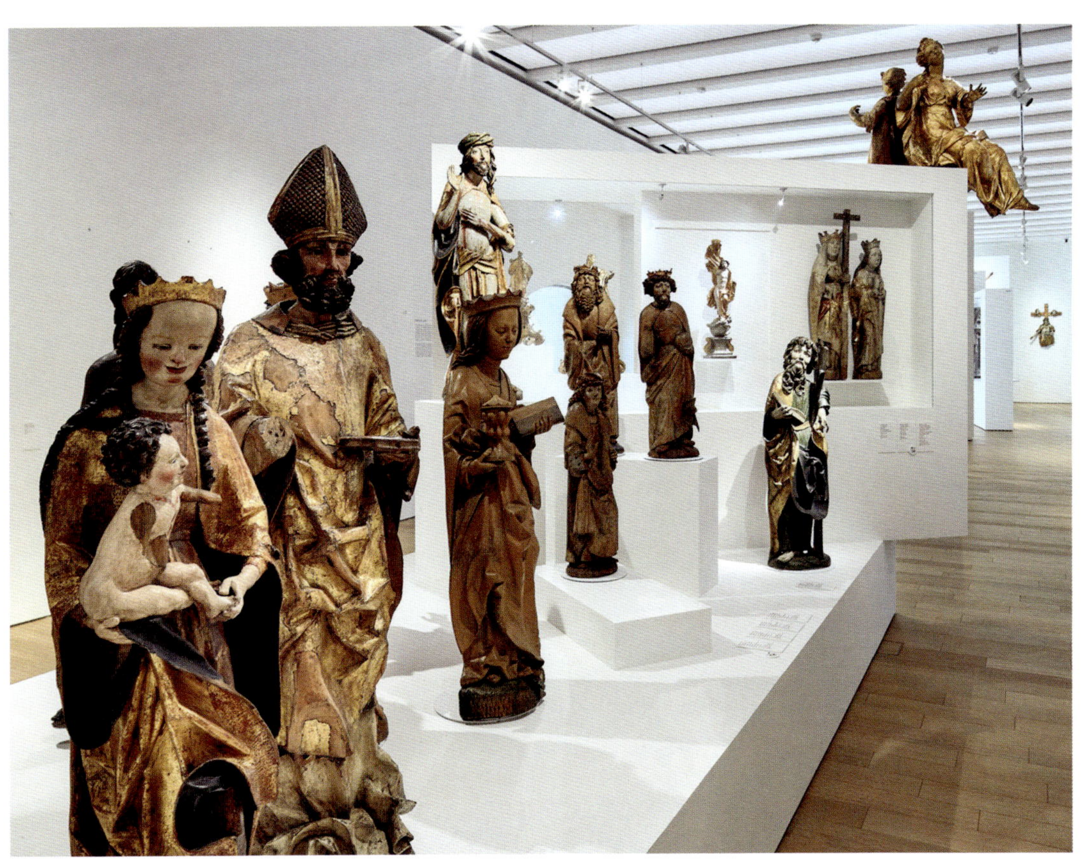

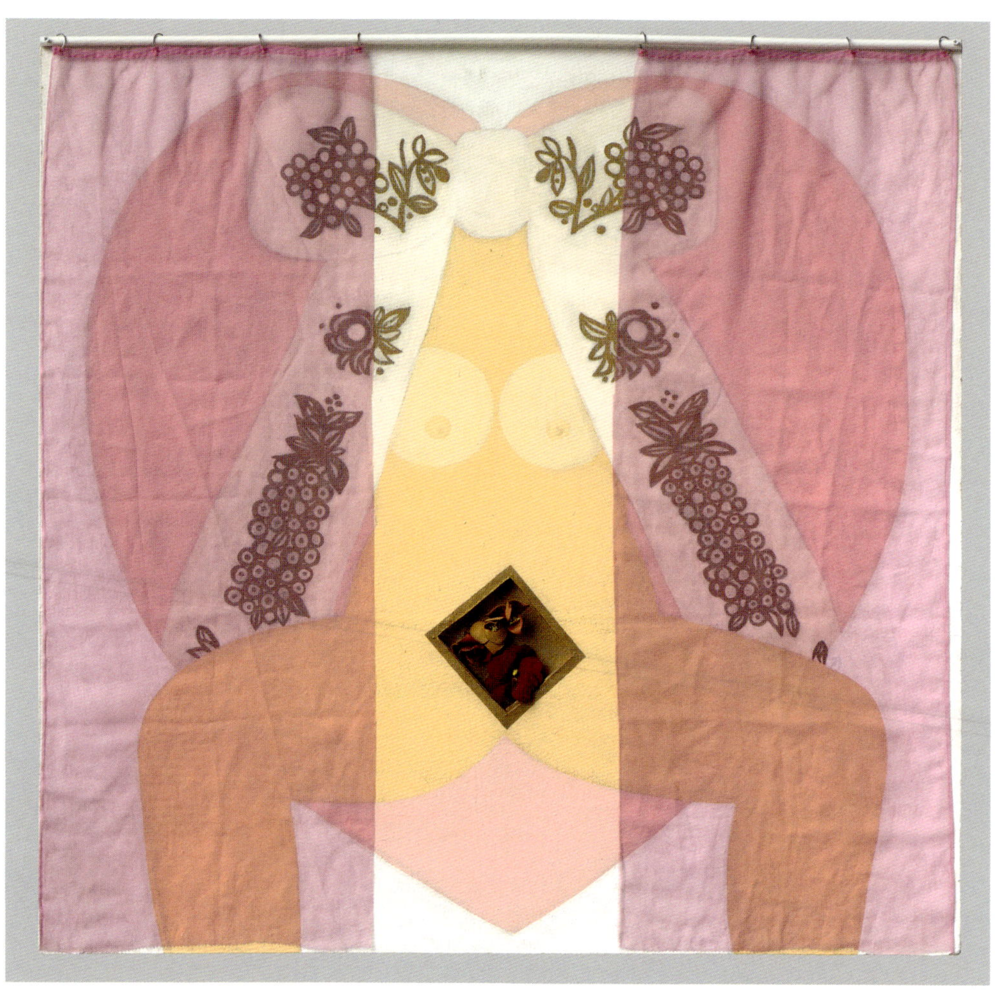

JANA ŽELIBSKÁ (born 1941)

Slovak Bride. 1967

Mixed media, 120 × 120 cm
Purchased in 2001. O 6813

I chose the work of this multimedia artist from the progressive generation of alternative Slovak performance and conceptual artists from the second half of the 1960s. Within our artistic scene, Želibská stood at the birth of environment and object, action and concept, postmodern object and installation, and video art. From the beginning her work has been provocative breaking stereotypes and taboos, even as her unconventional thinking and approach bring distinctive stimuli and values to our art scene. Although Želibská, with her interest in the themes of female physicality and intimacy, is often referred to as the first representative of feminist work in Slovakia, she herself relativises this position – justifiably so, because her scope is much broader. She addresses environmental issues (repeatedly returning to the themes of nature and ecology in various relationships in her work) and social criticism (of consumerism and media manipulation, for example), as well as experimenting with non-traditional, 'non-artistic' materials and means (light, sound, space and time within her objects and installations, combining image and music in video installations).

The work I chose beautifully portrays the atmosphere of the relaxed 1960s and is surprisingly sexually explicit by Slovak standards. What particularly appeals to me is the irreverence with which she handles our folkloric tradition, being both playful and (frighteningly) relevant, even today. Our colleague talks about a special kind of pop art in connection with this artist; in this case I think you can see why.

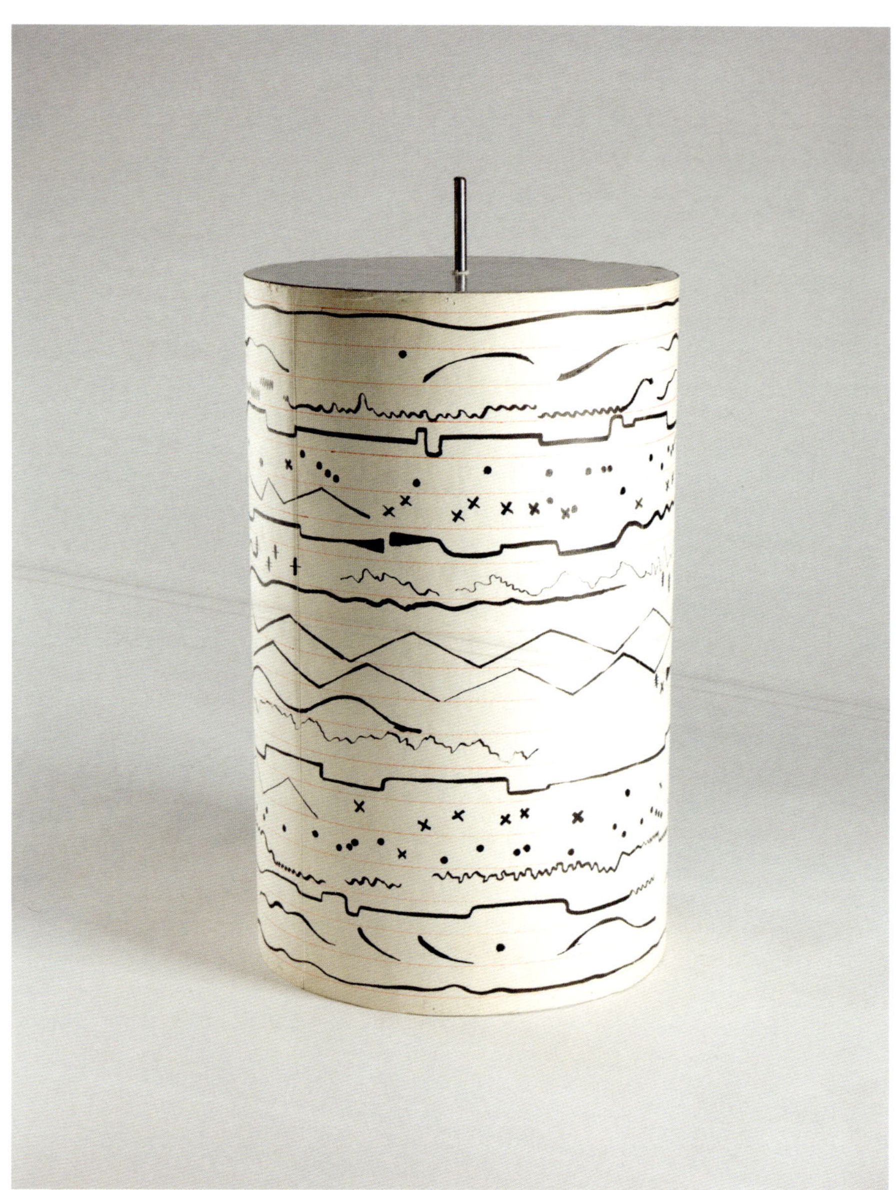

MILAN ADAMČIAK (1946–2017)

Three-Dimensional Score No. 3. 1969

Ink, marker on paper, 83 × 42 cm

Purchased in 1999. K 17644

The artist is an icon of Slovak neo-avant-garde art, a conceptual artist, author of visual poetry, musician, composer and musicologist. At home in two worlds, the musical and the visual, he used to say that he was interested in 'knowing a lot about something, and something about a lot'. Adamčiak built his authentic interdisciplinary and transdisciplinary programme on the intersection of science, music, poetry and the visual arts. He created an admirable body of work in the field of New Music, working in parallel with the Fluxus movement to invent and produce numerous original musical instruments, sound objects and acoustic environments. His graphic scores, conceived in an elaborate typology, are conceptual works of art. Yet they are also unconventional compositions, often interpreted by national and international musicians.

In 1989 Adamčiak founded *Transmusic comp.* together with Peter Machajdík and Michal Murín, an avant-garde ensemble with which they toured Europe. In 2017 we prepared an open-concept exhibition of his work in which, with the artist's input, we sought to present him personally and to showcase his multi-layered intermedia output from 1964 to date. The project unexpectedly changed direction when the author died two months before the opening. The exhibition thus became the first closed retrospective and the Slovak National Gallery became the codifier of the artist's legacy.

JOZEF SRNA, SR. (1930–1992)

Waning Sun – Self-Portrait. 1985

Oil on canvas, 150 × 120 cm

Purchased in 1985. O 6226

For many years, the work of this artist was automatically perceived as the art of socialist realism. Having been created at that time, and accurately portraying the surrounding world, it was sidelined after 1989 and marginalised as obsolete. Only now, more than 30 years after the revolution, are colleagues beginning to return to it. It was not error or ignorance; a certain distance is important for quality checking. In short, some things are more visible from afar. Our new interest lies not in the latent nostalgia obviously inherent in the paintings, but rather in its lucidity, a Chirico-like stillness, a quality created not by stopping and slowing down but by internalising and experiencing. The artist depicts a 'state of affairs', and the private, such as a self-portrait or a portrait of a family member, has a broader application. It affects its time, it captures a 'phenomenon'.

I chose the most representative painting in our collections: *Waning Sun.* This work has exactly the atmosphere described and at the same time it works as a parable, something not at all typical of the author. This work is his testimony. It is even a testimony against contemporary doctrine – the artist has placed himself in timelessness, out of space, out of context, sitting on a newspaper and leaning against a fence (from which side?), wearing formal trousers with creases combined with a proletarian vest, his pose remotely reminiscent of a crucifixion, with each individual object evoking an attribute. The title 'waning sun' may not relate to the weather at all; as it was the 1980s, it may refer to a worn-out ideology.

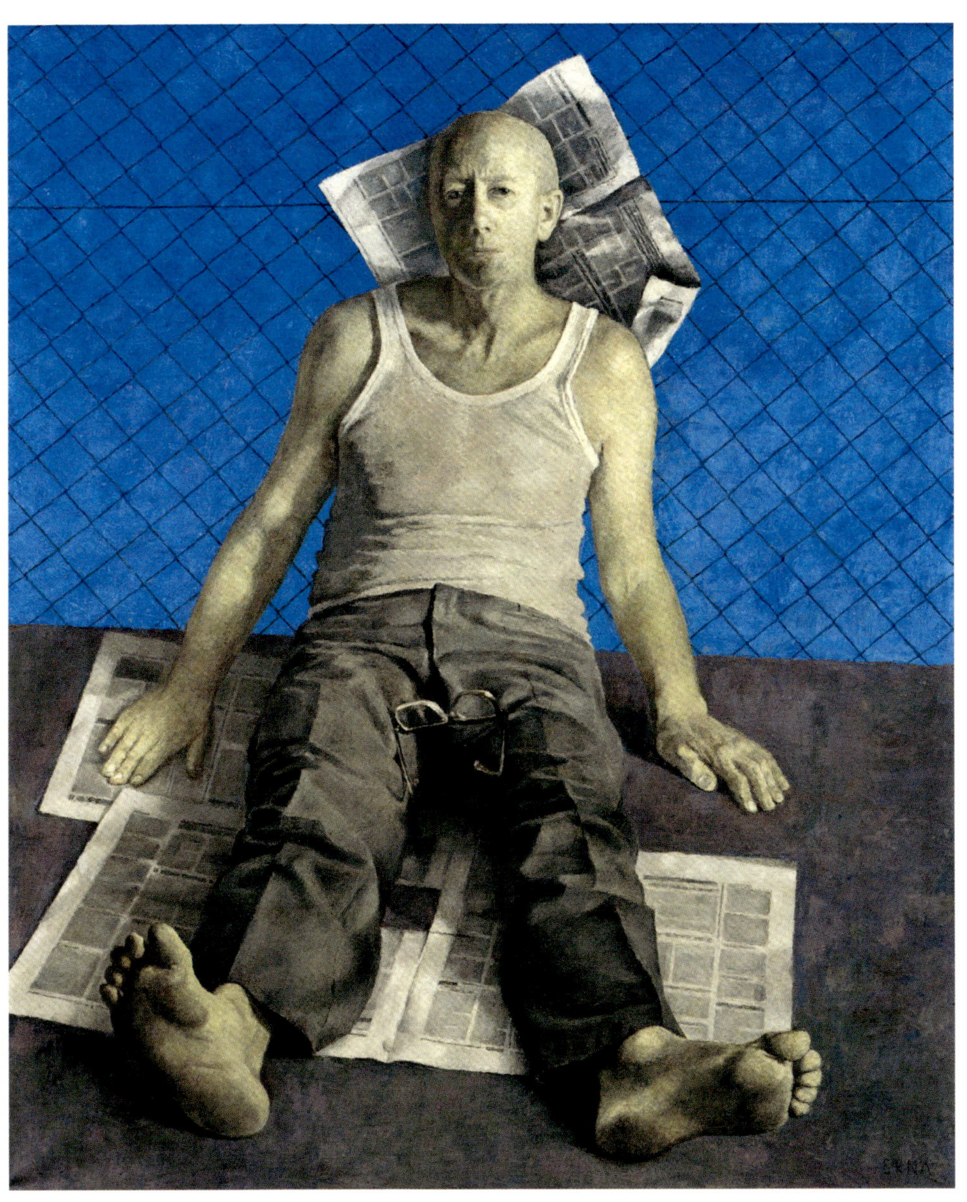

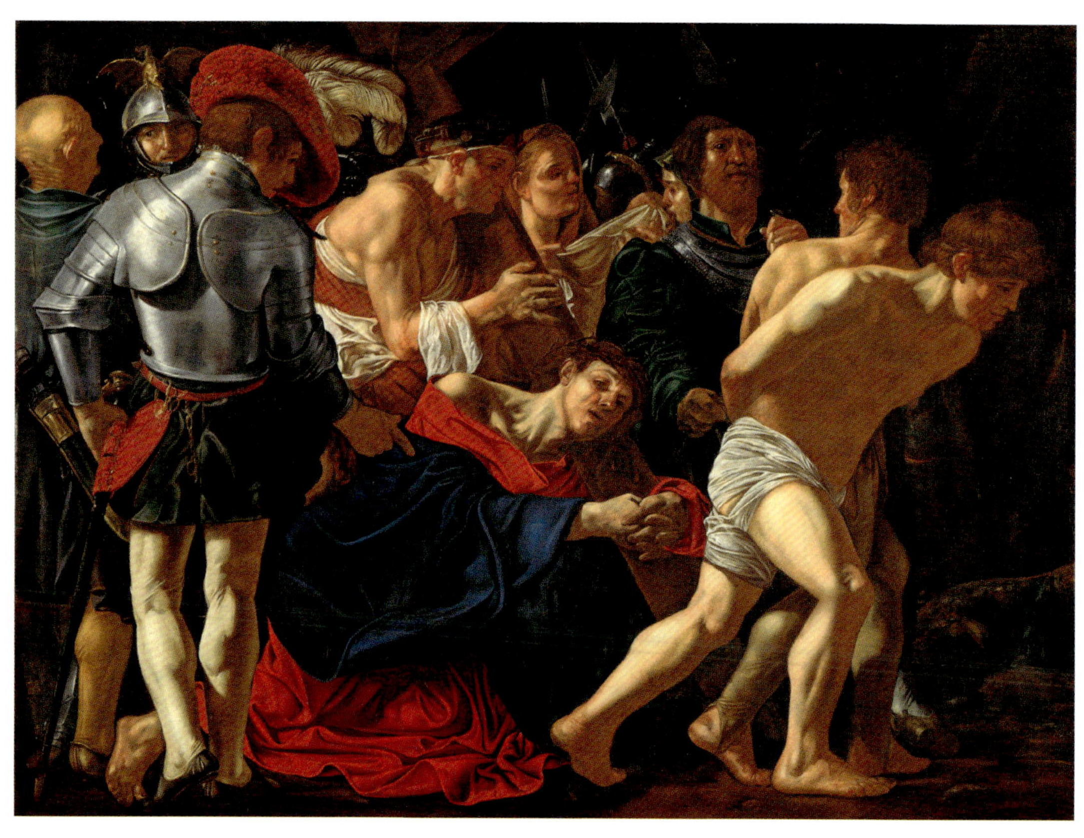

FRANCESCO BONERI, KNOWN AS CECCO DEL CARAVAGGIO
(1588/90–BEFORE 1630)

Christ Carrying the Cross. 1610–20

Oil on canvas, 98 × 130 cm (painting), 128 × 161 cm (frame)

Purchased in 1972. O 4175

The Slovak National Gallery was established late by European standards (1948), as if on a 'green meadow'. For that reason, its collection of European paintings does not match the volume of other European picture galleries, but it does contain some genuine jewels. One is *Christ Carrying the Cross* by the Italian baroque painter Francesco Boneri. As his artistic pseudonym suggests, he was deeply inspired by the work of the 'great' Caravaggio; in this respect he was one of a cohort of Caravaggio's pupils and followers.

His scene of the carrying of the cross, however, is conceived in a truly original way. While painters until that period had often repeated compositional formulas dating back to Martin Schongauer (late fifteenth century), Cecco produced an innovative composition: theatrically 'cramming' the entire group into a small space, he plunges the scene into darkness and allows contrasting light to model the half-naked bodies of both villains and helpers. In contrast, Christ is highlighted by colourful accents of drapery, his red dress and blue cloak. The scene was probably intense for the painter himself, so he muted its frontal attack by using a *repoussoir* figure – a soldier with his back turned to the viewer. Few paintings have such hypnotic subtlety. The specificity of the scene is enhanced by its actors being portrayed as ordinary people from everyday life. An interesting fact about this painting is that it is the greatest 'traveller' of our collections, being also the most loaned-out piece in our collection of early art.

ŠTEFAN PAPČO (born 1983)

Bivouac. 2008–10

Linden wood, 140 × 70 × 60 cm

Purchased in 2011. P 2711

The now iconic *Bivouac* sculpture entered the collections at a time when the Slovak National Gallery's purchasing policy had been curtailed for financial reasons. However, it was clear even then that this was an exceptional piece. The artist's more recent work only confirms this, particularly since from the outset he exhibited a rare homogeneity and focused integrity. This is evident not only in theme and environment, but also in formal treatment and inputs into new media – video art, action, installation and monumental projects of unconventional memorials. His works are grounded in a field that has so far given him unlimited possibilities; the starting point is mountaineering, overcoming obstacles and inaccessible places and the language of the environment and its community. More than merely an association of athletes at a time of unfreedom, this was the personification of an alternative and relatively free zone of existence. Papčo does not finish with creation of the sculpture, he begins. The sequence of processes that follows is important, when he personally carries works to inaccessible places in the mountains, lets the elements act on them and often documents their 'lives' with a time-lapse camera.

Our sculpture spent three years in the mountains, where it absorbed the 'gifts' of nature. Papčo has taken this theme further, casting some of the figures in bronze. By elevating them to a noble material, their formal resemblance to the homeless is suddenly conspicuous, naturally contributing to a further reading of the work. The Slovak Republic, through our institution, donated one of his statues to the UNESCO headquarters in Paris.

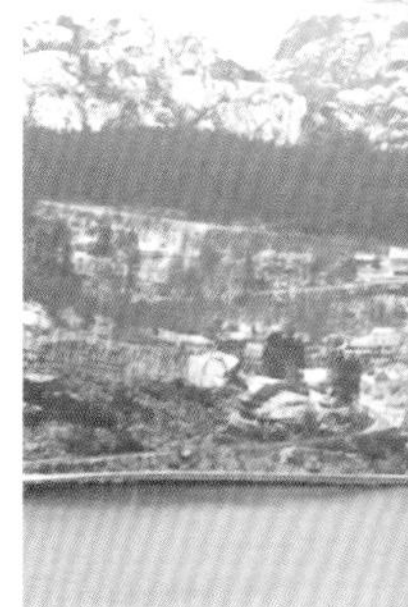

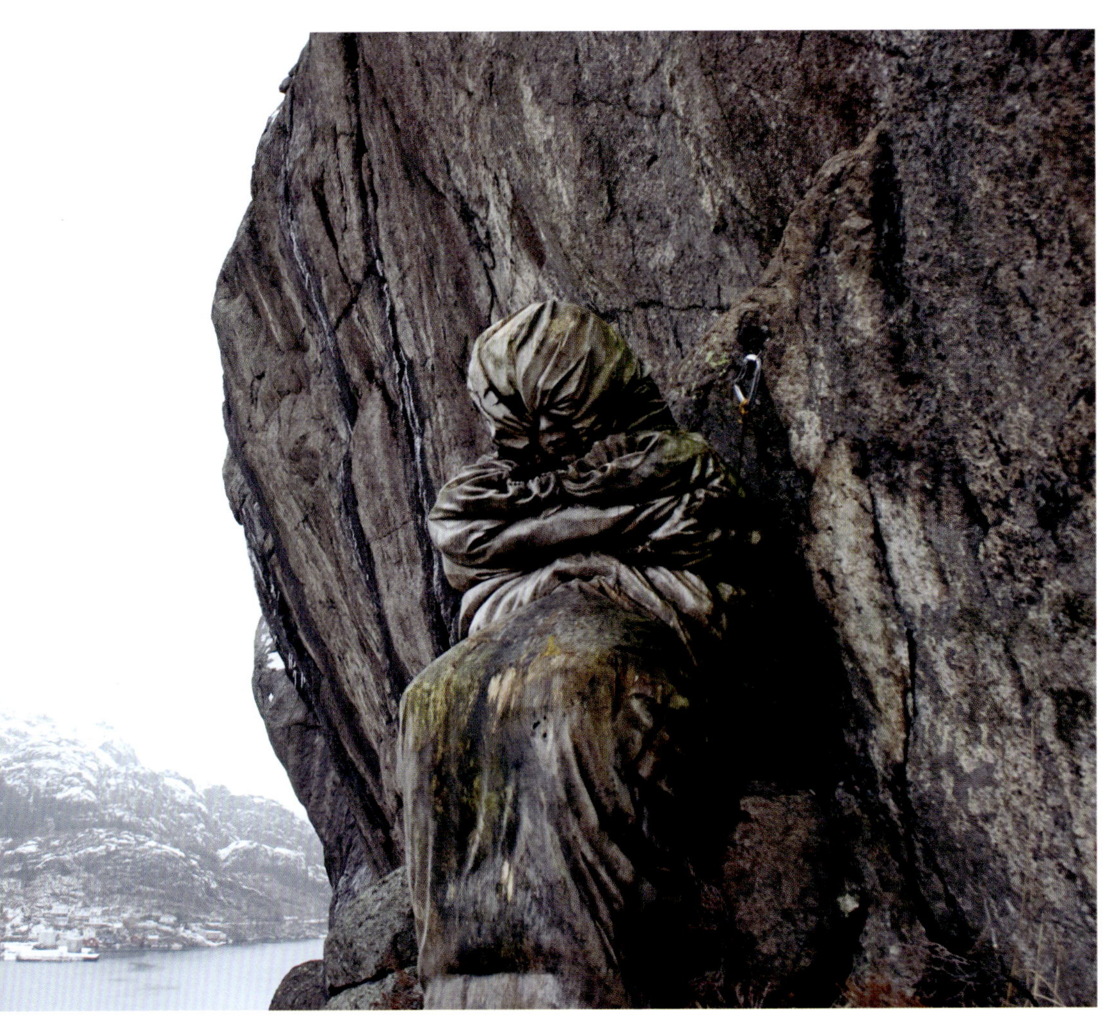

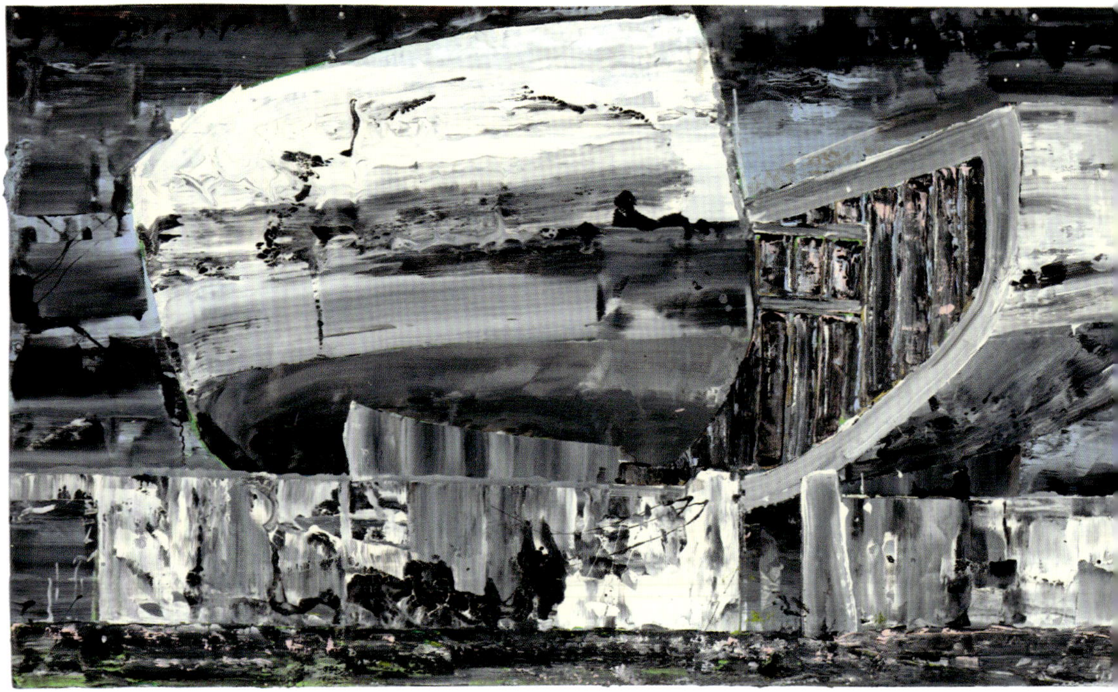

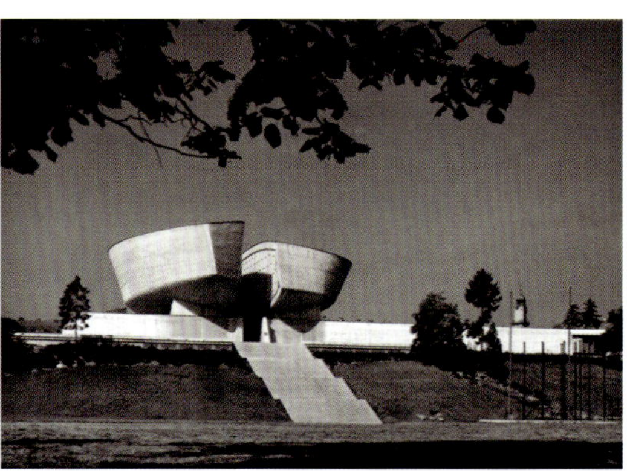

DUŠAN KUZMA (1927–2008):
Memorial to the Slovak National Uprising in Banská Bystrica. 1969 (collaboration Jozef Jankovič) Black and white photograph, 29.1 × 39.9 cm. Acquired as a purchase within the Rajmund Müller Archive (photo) in 2019. A 2296

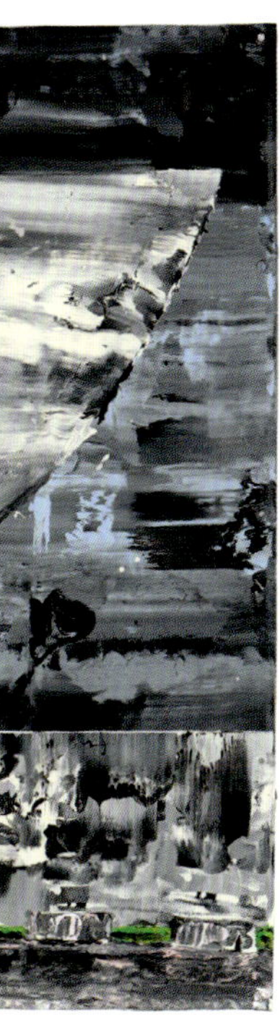

MATEJ FABIAN (born 1979)

Monument No. 1. 2012

Acrylic on banner fabric, 150 × 300 cm

Purchased in 2020. O 7192

In the new millennium, the Slovak art scene has been characterised by a strong inclination towards painting. In addition to inspiration from around the world, it is supported by good circumstances and a developing art market. However, Fabian is not an opportunist of this period. He is the author of a consistent artistic programme in which he renounces pop-like visual 'explorations' and returns to the basics of 'physical painting' and technological experimentation. In his work, he remains faithful to the examination of art history, or rather of art tradition, which he often associates with autobiographically chosen themes. Increasingly, Fabian creates objects or item paintings. For our gallery, for example, he created a Christmas tree, a *Wunderbaum* almost 3 metres in height.

The *Monument* painting was created during the period when the artist was working on his doctoral thesis – a painting experiment in which he processed the motif of a skull in various materials and techniques, from authorial experiments to restoration methods. The concept was the result of the painter's cumulative energy and his desire to conquer a larger dimension. Apart from its obvious painterly quality, the portrait of the Slovak National Uprising memorial speaks volumes about its architectural quality; in various ways it interprets the event better than many theoretical texts. In terms of Fabian's output, this work is clearly a *chef-d'oeuvre* – a 'happy painting' in which theme, execution and context are combined not only with autobiography, but also with an unexpectedly multi-layered interpretation, ranging from partisans to the symbolism of war as a macabre theme in art history.

ROMAN ONDAK (born 1966)

Sated Table. 1997

Ready-made, mixed media, height 140 cm
Purchased in 2000. P 2654

Roman Ondak is undoubtedly the best internationally known Slovak artist of our time, with his participatory installation *Measuring the Universe* (2007) crossing over into pop culture. He gained his reputation relatively soon after completing his artistic studies, since when he has regularly participated in relevant curatorial exhibitions and prepared monographic presentations around the world. Although his background is in conceptual art, he has repeatedly stressed that his 'things' refer to thinking about sculpture.

Ondak is concerned with the relationship between memory and image, playing with the substance, essence and dimension of the things he organises – and often invests with irony. His works hang between reality and utopia. The artist does not only work logically and analytically, but also involves the psychology of perception and is interested in the formula: perception – memory – thinking. Initially Ondak created material installations and more traditional objects, working with partially assisted ready-made items, mainly furniture, and intellectual writings ranging from philosophy to art theory. He would fill cabinets, a table or a display case with books doused in formaldehyde, or would glue simple typographic, even purist book covers of difficult-to-digest books onto canned food or food packaging.

This series also includes *Sated Table,* the artist's first exhibit in our collections. Although we now hold some of his more recent, better-known works, this is a reminder of the courage of our curators – in the circumstances of the time, the then 30-year-old Ondak was, despite his reputation, a bold choice.

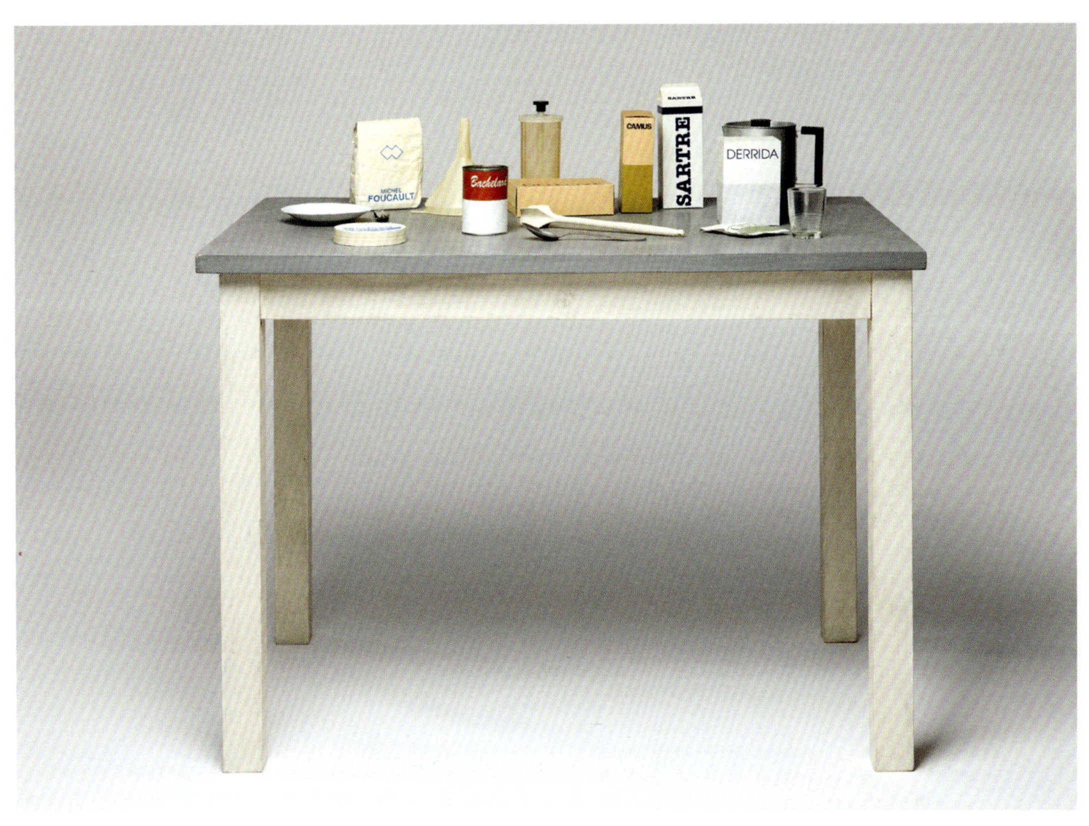

MICHEL
FOUCAULT
Bachelard
CAMUS
SARTRE
SARTRE
DERRIDA

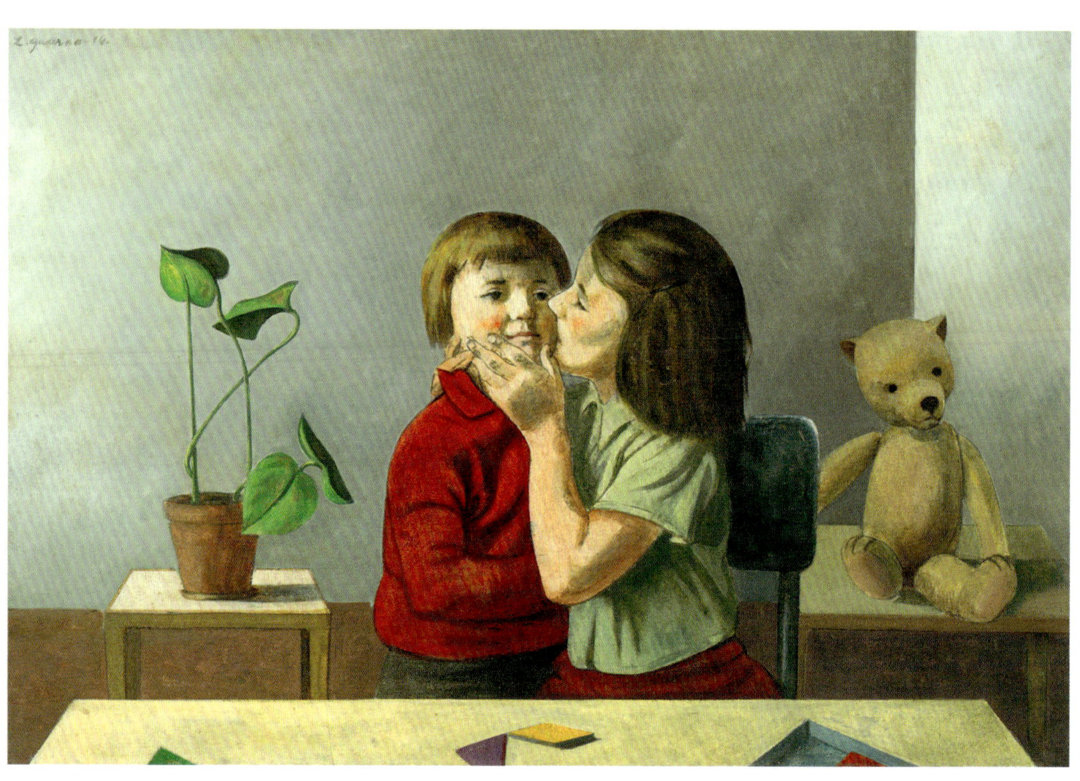

LADISLAV GUDERNA (1921–1999)

Little Girls. 1954

Tempera on plywood, 89 × 126.6 cm

Acquired as a transfer in 1958. O 1360

Guderna entered the art scene after the war as its *enfant terrible,* attracting well-deserved attention. This arrival was interrupted by communist cultural policy – he was no longer praised, but neither was he condemned. This curious image was created during the period of Stalinist socialist realism, but it is certainly not a typical example. Rather, it is a manifestation of how artists bred by modernism did not understand it. Despite widespread perception, this period did not abound with stylistic unity; in both painting and sculpture, artists created their own versions of socialist realism. They sought to find in them an expression of new realities, not by following Soviet models, but by drawing on domestic and individual artistic traditions. Many were confirmed leftists who did not doubt their own ideas, and their self-confidence defeated the Soviet models. They were not silent opponents of the regime; on the contrary, they held a respected position in the new structures.

Among them was Guderna, who learned from old masters, particularly the artists of the Italian Renaissance. At the time, the Renaissance was considered one of the 'good models'. As a reincarnated antiquity, it was a symbol of education and democracy – it represented the 'lost ideal' on which the 'new-born' society was to build. This approach was not based on the Soviet example, however, so the author's references to the Renaissance were disconcerting. Among the most successful is this painting, referring to Giotto's *Kiss of Judas* from the Cappella degli Scrovegni in Padua. I chose it not only for its strangely unsettling poetics, but also as a reminder of the great exhibition *Interrupted Song* (2012), devoted to the art of socialist realism, which was a public triumph.

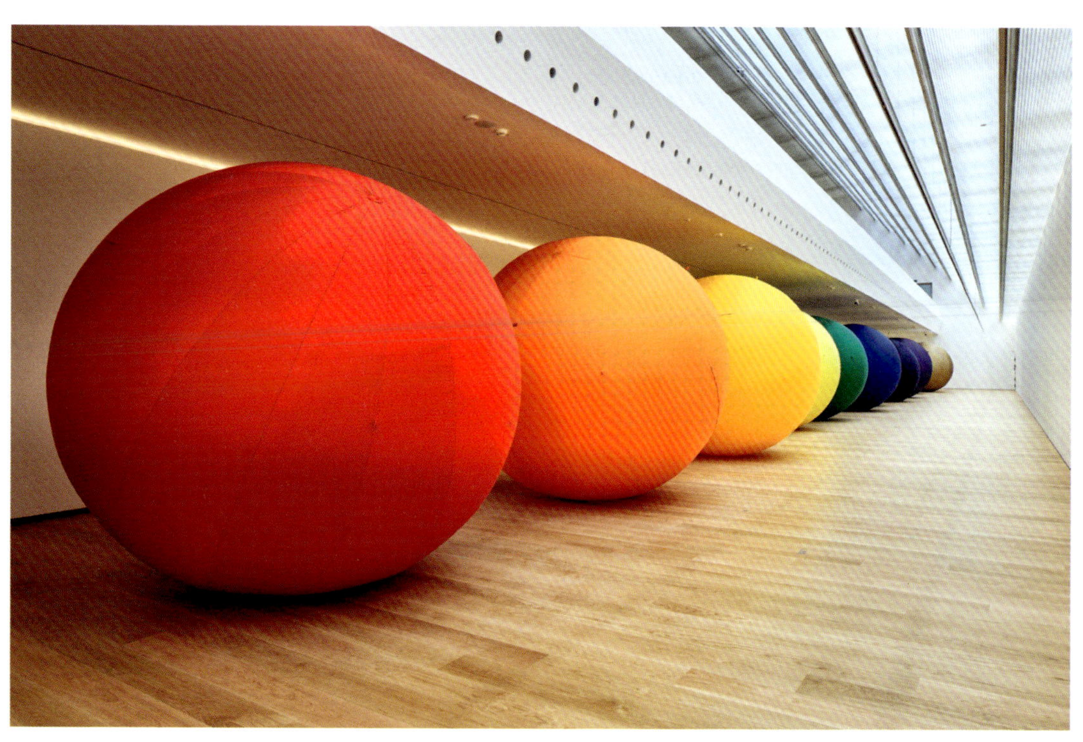

STANISLAV FILKO (1937–2015)

12 Colours of Reality – RETRQ = HAPPSOCSF. 2006.
1978–2011

Mixed media, balloons, engine

Acquired as a gift in 2014. IM 700/1-12

Filko is an internationally known neo-avant-garde artist who worked in Slovakia and in Düsseldorf, Germany – to where, as an established artist, he emigrated in 1982. From there he moved to New York, where he worked until 1990. Following the regime change, Filko returned to Czechoslovakia and worked intensively on the development of his universal cosmological concept, the System SF, within which he arranged his lifelong work according to concepts and colours. The installation is part of the project *12 Colours of Reality – RETRQ = HAPPSOCSF*, a continuation of the artist's earlier works from the series *HAPPSOC* – (happen society, *happening sociologique*). Filko, together with Alex Mlynárčik and Zita Kostrová, for the first time 'appropriated' places, everyday objects and parts of lived reality in the conceptual work *HAPPSOC I.* (1965), which they subsequently regarded as works of art. Not only did the artists creatively defy the totalitarian ideology controlling human lives, but they also extended perception of the artwork into the reality of everyday life.

The balloons, in the colours of the 12 chakras of Filko's original cosmological system, were originally designed for the outdoor environment of the Lyon Biennale in France in 2014. Within the exhibition hall, they more closely resemble metaphorical bodies, filling the newly opened building of the Slovak National Gallery with an entirely new breath and spirit. The set can also be exhibited individually. The work was exhibited indoors for the first time on the occasion of the opening of the Slovak National Gallery's reconstructed premises, immediately becoming our visual trademark. Following the 2023 murder in Bratislava of two young men because of their sexual orientation, the gallery's rainbow balloons took on a new context and a manifest urgency.

VLADIMÍR DEDEČEK (1929–2020)

Reconstruction and extension of the Slovak National Gallery.
1977 (project 1969)

Complex on the Bratislava waterfront. A 1631-36

The construction of our premises in the 1970s was an unexpectedly controversial event, even though in those days public criticism was harshly suppressed. The architect completed the baroque arcaded barracks on the Danube embankment to current urban scale and aesthetics. This clash of poetic arcades and large-scale sheet metal additions was a visual shock to most residents – a similar reaction to that experienced in Paris with the opening in 1977 of the Centre Pompidou (Renzo Piano, Richard Rogers). The design accords with the relationship between the city and the site, resulting in a set of buildings and public spaces. It is a structure that works with various communication links, such as passages, loggias, plateaus, terraces and covered walkways. The exhibition halls themselves, thanks to the bridge construction, are vast,

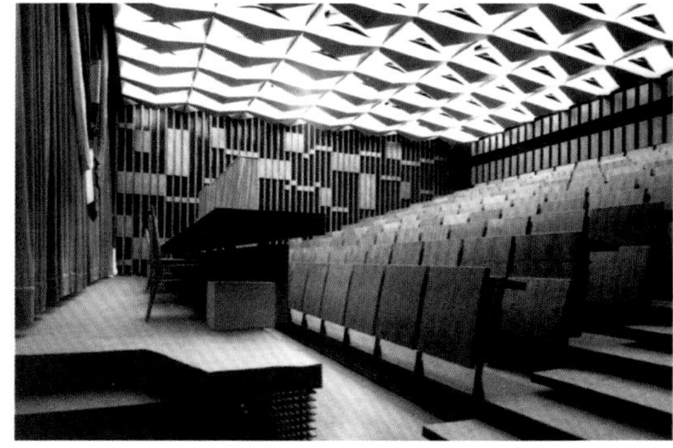

View of the cinema hall (1979).
Photograph. A 1631-102

well-lit individual rooms ready to be adapted to the needs of current exhibitions. It was probably the white and red aluminium cladding that, following the regime change in 1989, provoked outrage and public clamouring for demolition of the building.

In 2001, discussions around the Slovak National Gallery's future were 'won' by its users and talk of reconstruction began. In 2005 a design by architects Martin Kusý and Pavel Paňák won the public competition, and a convoluted process led to the gallery eventually opening to the public in 2022. The situation with the building has defined and determined our activities for many years – as a work of true signature architecture, it is also the largest object in our collection.

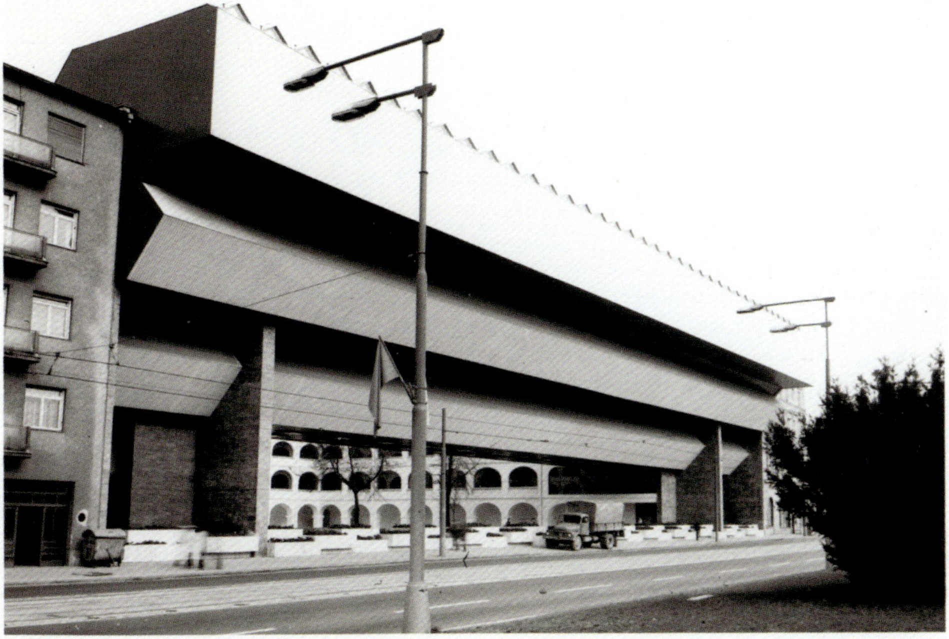

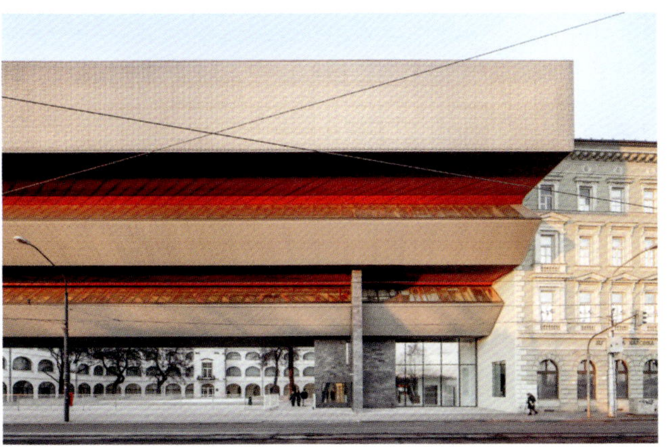

MARTIN KUSÝ, PAVOL PAŇÁK:
Reconstruction, extension and modernisation of the Slovak National Gallery. 2022
(project 2007)

First published in 2024 by
Scala Arts & Heritage Publishers Ltd
43 Great Ormond Street, London WC1N 3HZ, UK
www.scalapublishers.com
An imprint of B. T. Batsford Holdings Ltd.

In association with the Slovak National Gallery
Riečna 1, Bratislava 815 13, Slovak Republic

ISBN (Scala) 978-1-78551-574-3
ISBN (SNG) 978-80-8059-278-3

Translation from Slovak: Beata Bradford
Project managers: Kateřina Siegl and Beth Holmes (Scala), Miroslava Plesníková (SNG)
Supervising editor: First Edition Translations Ltd, Cambridge, UK (Scala), Luďka Kratochvílová (SNG)
Designed by: Jana Bálik
Printed in Turkey

10 9 8 7 6 5 4 3 2 1

COOPERATION ON TEXTS:
Ján Abelovský (*Anton Jasusch*)
Katarína Bajcurová (*Martin Benka, Jozef Jankovič, Milan Laluha*)
Vladimíra Büngerová (*Maria Bartuszová, Roman Ondak, Štefan Papčo*)
Dušan Buran (*Jakub Bogdan, Expozícia sakrálneho umenia*)
Lucia Gregorová Stach (*Milan Adamčiak, Stano Filko, Marcel Mališ*)
Petra Hanáková (*Marko Blažo, Lucia Nimcová, Emília Rigová*)
Alexandra Homoľová (*Stano Filko, Franz Anton Palko, Jana Želibská*)
Aurel Hrabušický (*Šymon Kliman, Martin Kollar, Július Koller, Viliam Malík, Martin Martinček*)
Viera Kleinová (*Jozef Sušienka*)
Monika Mitášová (*Anna Daučíková*)

THANKS:
Lucia Almášiová, Katarína Beňová, Denis Haberland, Petra Hanáková, Katarína Kolbiarz Chmelinová, Zuzana Ludiková for publication proposals

FRONT COVER:
STANISLAV FILKO:
12 Colours of Reality – RETRO = HAPPSOCSF. 2006. 1978–2011

BACK COVER:
MARTIN KUSÝ, PAVOL PAŇÁK:
Detail from the soffit of the SNG Bridge façade. 2022

FRONTISPIECE:
ĽUDOVIT GODE: *Melancholy.* 1770–1790 (artwork located in the SNG entrance hall)

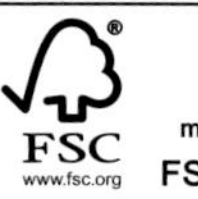